THE
Charleston
Bulletin
SUPPLEMENTS

THE
Charleston Bulletin
SUPPLEMENTS

VIRGINIA WOOLF
& QUENTIN BELL

Edited and with an introduction
by Claudia Olk

THE BRITISH LIBRARY

FRONTISPIECE   Front cover of the Supplement 'The Messiah'

First published in 2013 by
The British Library
96 Euston Road
London NW1 2DB

© in Introduction, 2013 Claudia Olk
© in the Charleston Bulletin Supplements, text and images,
2013 the Estates of Virginia Woolf and Quentin Bell
© in Preface, 2013 David Bradshaw

All illustrations from The British Library
except those on pp. x, 9, 12 & 15, which are © Tate, London 2013

British Library Cataloguing-in-Publication Data
A catalogue record for this book is available from The British Library
ISBN   978 0 7123 5891 0

Designed and typeset in Monotype Joanna by illuminati, Grosmont
Printed in Hong Kong by Great Wall Printing Co. Ltd

Contents

Preface

IN MAY 1923 Leonard Woolf was made literary editor of *The Nation and Atheneum*, a heavyweight journal that issued occasional specialist supplements of great sobriety and authority. Later that year his wife, Virginia, in collaboration with her young nephew, Quentin Bell, began to produce these no less occasional but utterly frolicsome *Charleston Bulletin* Supplements. The *Bulletin* ran to many issues between 1923 and 1927, a span of years that coincides with Woolf's excited discovery of the vision, technique and confidence, following the breakthrough achievement of *Jacob's Room* (1922), to write *Mrs Dalloway* (1925) and *To the Lighthouse* (1927). While the dominant mood of the Supplements can be more closely (if very loosely) connected with such off-piste works as the fantastic *Orlando* (1928) and the whimsical *Flush* (1933), it doesn't seem too ridiculous to link their skittish abandon with the continuing sense of liberation Woolf experienced in the wake of *Jacob's Room*. Even so, she rarely wrote in a more zany or carefree spirit, or with such an intimate sense of her audience, as she did when she penned these slight but delightful in-house sketches.

The Supplements' giddy energy perfectly reflects the skimble-skamble milieu of Charleston, the Sussex farmhouse where Vanessa Bell, her two sons Julian and Quentin, her daughter Angelica, Duncan Grant and David Garnett had lived in bohemian and mostly fruitful harmony since 1916, and where other members of the Bloomsbury Group, notably Clive Bell (Julian and Quentin's father), Roger Fry, Mary Hutchinson,

Lytton Strachey, Desmond and Molly MacCarthy, and the Woolfs spent many a talkative sojourn or made many a gossipy visit. At one level, therefore, the ephemerality of the Supplements could not more perfectly capture the stream of chatter, pranks and joshing that were a key element of Charleston's life-blood, with Woolf's sister Vanessa 'presid[ing] over the most astonishing ménage: Belgian hares, governesses, children, gardeners, hens, ducks, and painting all the time, till every inch of the house is a different colour', as Woolf put it in a letter of May 1919. A great deal of serious thinking about art and life also took place at Charleston, but the Supplements tend to portray it as a slapstick realm of hilarious upheavals, sudden explosions, zany mishaps and paint-bespattered foggy-mindedness.

The impression of Woolf we pick up from these Supplements could not be more at odds with the view of her we are presented with in a film such as *The Hours*, where she is played as a fey, *distraite* and vulnerable figure who is far too rarefied and delicate to indulge in any kind of horseplay with her young relations. Yet even the most cursory reading of her diaries and letters reveals a woman with a sharp lampoonist's eye and an almost adolescent relish for scabrous and scatological titbits; a writer who took the greatest delight in monkey business and the sheer absurdity of life. Similarly, many of her novels also reveal her skill as a satirist and this spirit is also conspicuous in the Supplements, where she is especially adept at poking fun at Clive Bell. As a young woman, Woolf had been susceptible to his aesthetic charm, but as she matured her personal writings record her increasing exasperation with her brother-in-law's self-absorbed antics. In 'Eminent Charlestonians' she gently mocks Clive's premature 'depilation of the scalp' by suggesting that his baldness 'supervened upon the discovery of the infestation by Lepidoptera of his second best suit of evening clothes', whereas in 'The Messiah' she proposes that 'his comparative epidermic depilation in later life' may have been caused by lady admirers stealing locks of his hair for their 'reticules' when he was a young man in Wiltshire. Duncan Grant's legendary vagueness receives similar treatment in 'The Dunciad', while in the Supplements as a whole family history, farmhouse mythology and all manner of Bloombury tittle-tattle is turned into humorous copy by the Group's most keen-eyed and irreverent chronicler.

In one vignette we glimpse an omnivorous camel on the rampage in Fitzroy Street and in others Vanessa Bell eats her beads rather than her porridge and Duncan Grant sets fire to the Charleston pond (killing three flying fish, three porpoises, one whale, a tinned sardine and many other creatures in the process). And although it would be much too heavy-handed to claim that such nonsensical flights of fancy as 'The Life and Death History of a Studio' were inspired by Lewis Carroll or Edward Lear, their spirits dance over the Supplements. It is also worth asking, as Woolf gradually fashioned her greatest, ghost-haunted, ghost-laying family novel, To the Lighthouse, whether these Supplements acted as an off-beat channel through which she carried herself back to the world of her early years? As young girls, she and Vanessa, along with their brother Thoby, had produced the Hyde Park Gate News (1891–95), and since the Charleston Bulletin Supplements also revolve around family jokes, stories and leg-pulling, was there, perhaps, something more nostalgic at play in her readiness to write these sketches with her nephew? Was there something in the sheer puerility of the Supplements that helped her to rekindle the mood of the Hyde Park newspaper and so bring her even closer to the ghostly crucible of her childhood?

Some of the Supplements' in-jokes are difficult to prise open, but for others we have letters and diary entries that offer illuminating sidelights. In the summer of 1927, for instance, the

Woolfs bought their first car, a Singer, while Vanessa acquired a second-hand Renault. 'Monthly Calendar' alludes to the death of a cat and the near fatality of a boy that ensued when the sisters took their cars on the roads, while the deeper and more complex rivalries between Charleston and Monks House (where the Woolfs lived nearby), which these cars came to symbolise, is depicted in Quentin's sketch of the machines nose to nose. 'But impartial observers were unanimously of opinion that the SINGER WAS THE BEST', Woolf cannot prevent herself scribbling.

'My Bell family relations are young, fertile & intimate', Woolf wrote in her diary in 1930. 'Julian & Quentin change so much. This year Q. is shabby easy natural & gifted; last year he was foppish, finicky & affected.' As these clusters of adjectives indicate, Woolf took a zealous and calibrated interest in every stage of Quentin's development and she followed his growth into manhood with absorbed affection. While it might be tempting for some readers to forge a deep-down connection between their lively collaboration on these Charleston squibs and the childless Woolf's occasional sense of the incompleteness of her own household, the sketches are best read solely in the spirit in which they were first created: 'fertile & intimate' trifles that were concocted in an instant simply to amuse.

PROFESSOR DAVID BRADSHAW

OXFORD UNIVERSITY

OVERLEAF   Quentin Bell, Virginia and Leonard Woolf

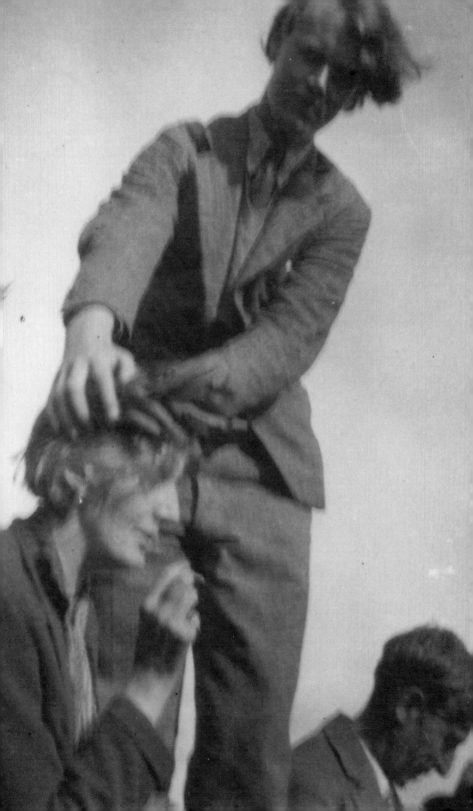

Introduction

IN THE SUMMER of 1923 Quentin Bell and his elder brother Julian founded a family newspaper, *The Charleston Bulletin*:

> My brother and I produced a family newspaper; it was daily.
> I made all the illustrations and most of the other matter.
> From time to time my brother got bored and stopped work.
> I carried on reporting and inventing the news as best I could
> until he, exasperated by my spelling, my handwriting, my
> grammar etc, would take over again. Thus it happened that I
> asked for a contribution from my aunt Virginia. I knew she
> was an author, and although I didn't think much of her work
> – that is to say I had failed to finish *Kew Gardens* – it seemed
> stupid to have a real author so close at hand and not have her
> contribute.[1]

Quentin Bell succeeded, and his aunt Virginia Woolf did indeed contribute to the newspaper. But instead of occasionally providing articles or essays, she joined forces with Quentin, and from 1923 until 1927 they created more fully fledged special issues, booklets of stories and drawings that were announced as Supplements. Written or dictated by Woolf and illustrated by Quentin Bell, these *Charleston Bulletin* Supplements present a unique kind of collaboration between the young nephew and the novelist during her most prolific years, when she wrote and published works such as *Mrs Dalloway* (1925), *The Common Reader* (1925) and *To the Lighthouse* (1927).

In Virginia Woolf, Quentin Bell found not only a professional author and an experienced journalist, who by the time they started collaborating had become a famous public figure, but,

Charleston Farm, postcard owned by Grace Higgens

above all, a close companion and conspirator who shared his irreverence and more often than not his mischievous sense of humour. Woolf, who spent many summers in Monk's House, Rodmell, close to Charleston Farmhouse where Quentin lived with his family and their various house guests during his holidays, refers to their common enterprise when one of her letters closes in the amused remark: 'Please consider our summer libel'.[2] Their alliance was built on mutual inspiration and surreptitious exchanges, but it was also tinged by a latent mock-rivalry between the arts of writing and painting. On 6 May 1928, after several years of collaboration, Woolf writes:

> My dear Quentin, Your letter has been rather a surprise to me; because if you can write as well as all that, with such abandonment to devilry and ribaldry, – for I don't believe a word of what you say – how in Gods name can you be content to remain a painter? Surely you must see the infinite superiority of the language to the paint? Think how many

things are impossible in paint; giving pain to the Keynes', making fun of one's aunts, telling libidinous stories, making mischief – these are only a few of the advantages; against which a painter has nothing to show: for all his merits are also a writer's. Throw up your career, for God's sake.[3]

Quentin Bell, however, did not choose to follow his aunt's advice. He remained faithful to his desire to become an artist and later found himself as a professor of art history and an art critic. Nevertheless, he never abandoned writing, and, among his many other works, wrote the first biography of his aunt.

Quentin Bell's practical and tactical move to take advantage of having an author in the family was founded on the close friendship between him and his aunt, which developed into a long-term collaboration. 'Will you tell Quentin,' Woolf writes to her sister Vanessa in 1926, 'I would like to come and see him, and we will certainly publish a book together,'[4] and in the Preface to *Orlando*, she acknowledges Quentin Bell as 'an old and valued collaborator in fiction'. It is this spirit of collaboration, the two of them sparking each other off in inventing stories and creating imaginary lives, that the *Charleston Bulletin* Supplements preserve and thrive on.

The Supplements that this edition presents for the first time, and that are very likely the last remaining of Virginia Woolf's unpublished works, are part of the larger enterprise that constitutes the *Charleston Bulletin*. Modelled on the *Hyde Park Gate News*, the family newspaper written by the Stephen children, Vanessa, Thoby and Virginia, from 1891 until 1895,[5] the *Charleston Bulletin*, according to Quentin Bell 'consciously imitated the early efforts at journalism of my Aunt Virginia and her siblings',[6] thus continued the tradition of the family journal into the next generation. The *Charleston Bulletin* was launched by the 'Charleston Bulletin Press' when the editor, Julian, and the illustrator, Quentin, were aged fifteen and thirteen respectively,

Julian and Clive Bell

and the newspaper lived on, as the *New Bulletin*, with numerous interruptions, until the end of 1927.

Quentin eventually took over the role of editor, and the *Bulletin* was written or printed, i.e. typed, in the early morning and presented to the family at breakfast:[7] 'As Editor,' writes Quentin, 'I rose at 5.30 am to get it written and delivered at breakfast – not the habit of a lazy child!'[8] The *Bulletin* chronicles daily events and provides a weather report, accounts of explorations in nature, records of comings and goings, and the many great and small adventures in and around the household.

Like the daily *Bulletin*, the special Supplements were created for private circulation at Christmas and became a vehicle for family jokes. Designed to tease the adults, they portrayed

Quentin Bell

Bloomsbury eccentricities along with the foibles and mishaps of the residents and visitors at Charleston. Their coverage was also extended beyond Charleston itself and included the Keyneses at nearby Tilton farmhouse, known as the 'Tiltonians'[9] or 'The Squire and his lady', the 'Woolves', or Rodmellians, at Rodmell, and friends and acquaintances of the household in London, Cassis and St Tropez.

The close nature of their collaboration, in which Woolf's text and her nephew's sketches are delicately interlaced, makes it difficult to determine whether the text or the illustration came first. Rather text and image enter into a relation that is expressive of the ways in which Woolf and Bell mutually inspired each other. Hence, in some instances the text describes

Quentin, Angelica
and Julian

the image, whereas in others the image illustrates the text, and
in yet others the illustration, such as that of a chamber pot with
a pattern reminiscent of the Omega workshop's designs, is left
to speak for itself: 'This scene had better be imagined than
described it is enough to say that the article was white with a
greek key pattern in orange'.

In their minimalist, episodic form the Supplements create
an equivalent to both a family album and a child's sketchbook.
They were presented to the adults on special occasions such
as Christmas, and they were received benevolently. Vanessa
Bell, after having obtained the supplement about her 'Life' on
Christmas Day 1923 writes to her sister: 'I am almost more
overcome by my own life than by anything else, however.
Not a single word of it's true of course but I admit it made me

laugh and the pictures are really lovely.'[10] In their subtle humour and their playfully mocking tone the Supplements engage an active audience that more often than not was the target of their wicked jokes. Virginia Woolf clearly enjoyed writing the stories and hearing about how they were received. Thus she enquires about whether 'The Dunciad', the life of Duncan Grant, which was written for Christmas 1924, went down well with its readers: 'Was the Dunciad a success? I have some ideas for a new one, tell Quentin.'[11] Vanessa Bell herself took great interest in the development of the Bulletin, and although she did not directly contribute, she helped to procure stories for it. She writes to Roger Fry:

> By the way, your story about me was unfortunately lost before it could be published, [in the Charleston Bulletin] so we have never known it. Quentin read it but can't remember the exact words, which he says are important. If it's not too much trouble do send it again, to me this time. The Bulletin has been very much to the fore lately. Large numbers appear every day and its journalese is becoming very brilliant.[12]

Like its predecessor, the Hyde Park Gate News, the Charleston Bulletin ties family history to a place that is representative of a way of life.[13] Virginia Woolf, when in London misses Charleston and 'the whole atmosphere of ragamuffin delight',[14] and Virginia Nicholson, Vanessa's granddaughter, recalls that 'Charleston was a place where, for both children and adults, messy creativity was a way of life.'[15] In a letter to Helen Anrep, Roger Fry describes the Charleston Bulletin as a lively part of Charleston's overall ease and energy:

> This is the most peaceful domestic existence conceivable; there's only Clive, Vanessa and the children. It might be held up as a model of what family life ought to be. The extraordinary thing is that the two boys amuse themselves wildly with almost nothing particular to do. ... They spend

the whole evening concocting the News Bulletin which appears at breakfast the next morning generally typewritten. It contains a fantastic version of the daily events, generally very much to Vanessa's discredit – a good many satirical and comic poems illustrated by Quentin, and a weather prophecy.[16]

Charleston was by no means a typical household. Decorated by Vanessa Bell and Duncan Grant, it was a place of creativity which both embodied and resisted domesticity. The farmhouse was first spotted by Leonard Woolf in 1916[17] and subsequently leased by Vanessa Bell in the autumn of the same year. It became the Sussex home to her and her children and also to her friend and lover Duncan Grant and to David Garnett, both of whom worked on a nearby farm to avoid conscription. Before long, it served as a hospitable retreat to many Bloomsbury residents and visitors. The most frequent among these were Clive Bell, John Maynard and Lydia Keynes, Virginia and Leonard Woolf, as well as Lytton Strachey, Desmond and Molly MacCarthy, Mary Hutchinson and Roger Fry.

Charleston represented a microcosm where art and life had become interpenetrating realities, and despite the vicissitudes of life, the wartime tribulations and domestic upheavals, the household retained its vigour and magnetism. At times this led to it being inundated by self-invited visitors in need of entertainment who 'stayed hours and had nothing to say',[18] so that Vanessa was prompted on occasion to put up a noticeboard at the bottom of the hill saying: 'Charleston. OUT'.[19]

Frances Partridge, a long-term friend of the family, describes her first visit: 'I can only evoke the impression I got on first entering the hall as a visitor – the strong feeling of life being intensely and purposefully lived, of animated talk, laughter, brilliant colour everywhere, youth.'[20] Youth indeed seems to be a key term to describe the spirit of Charleston as

Portrait of the editor
capturing two
new subscribers:
Quentin Bell with
Lydia and John
Maynard Keynes

an environment that was both intimate and liberating, one
that exuded liveliness and resourcefulness and retained a sense
of improvisation and renewal, where nothing was built for
eternity, and where walls and furniture could be, and indeed
were, painted over and over again.

The collaborations between Virginia Woolf, Quentin and
Julian Bell capture this spirit of openness and invention, of
upsetting conventions and deflating highbrow artistic gravitas
in the episodes of the Supplements to the *Charleston Bulletin*.
The Supplements present selections of incidents in the lives of
the adults that are built around significant scenes and brief but
telling moments. Virginia Woolf's sparkling wit pervades her
style of writing which is limpid, succinct, richly allusive and
highly ironic. Some of the stories also gain poetic licence from

Vanessa Bell
with Angelica

the child's point of view and provide fresh and unobtrusive insights into the Bloomsbury of the 1920s. Occurrences that were scarcely noticed by the 'Charlestonians' were all the more keenly recorded by Woolf and Quentin Bell. Beneath the pitiless eye of the collaborators, ordinary experience unfolds into mock-epic forms such as the satiric apocalypse of Duncan Grant's life in 'The Dunciad', the quasi-biblical life of Clive Bell in 'The Messiah of Bloomsbury', or enchanted encounters like the one between Vanessa Bell and a camel.

The Supplements present fantastical narrative excursions into family history. They evoke imaginary details and build up fictional personalities. The writer and the illustrator are united in their dislike of seriousness and boredom and they mercilessly target shallowness and hypocrisy. Their accounts are peppered with jokes and interspersed with literary allusions as they ironically draw on such models as Pope's *Dunciad*, Lytton Strachey's *Eminent Victorians*, and Handel's *Messiah*.

The Supplements are pervaded by the spell of Vanessa Bell's presence, and among all the characters that appear it is Vanessa who emerges as the heroine of many of the tales. The 'Christmas Supplement of 1923', written in the hand of the thirteen-year-old Quentin Bell, is entirely devoted to 'Scenes from the life of Vanessa Bell'. Many of the scenes that retell events from her childhood, praise her free spirit and her unconventional, exploring mind, while, at the same time, wryly commenting on the ways in which her natural curiosity habitually defies the laws of time and gravity: 'Scene 10: Heris Nessa washing her hands in a Turkish well and seein if her ring will float – they do not'. Vanessa appears strong-willed, candid and adventurous, but, being an artist, she is satirically portrayed as slightly at odds with conventional reality. Poised but occasionally absent-minded, she is surrounded by decomposing arrangements for still-lives, and her idiosyncratic sense of time, a characteristic that she shares with Duncan Grant, more than once baffles her friends: 'Well said Duncan, if that clock has been an hour Fast or 2 slow we might quite well have been in the train by now. Its a mere matter of time said Nessa.' The 'Life of Vanessa Bell' renders her succinct wit and also her habit of mixing up proverbs when it reports that on her wedding day she gets lost in London and misses the train to her honeymoon destination in Wales because the chauffeur had 'lost his way like a needle in a camels eye as Nessa said'.

Next to Vanessa Bell, Duncan Grant and Clive Bell are the most prominent Charlestonians to feature in the Supplements. The Life of Clive Bell, 'The Messiah of Bloomsbury', appears as the Christmas Supplement of 1925. It presents the 'nativity' in Clive Bell's family's Wiltshire manor, in the presence of stuffed

Duncan Grant,
E.M. Forster, Clive
Bell and Mary
Hutchinson in the
walled garden

hunting trophies substituting the real ox and ass, and it records
his first expression of artistic talent and taste when he banishes
his nurse's display of Christmas cards at the age of six. The
'Messiah' chronicles Clive's arrival at Cambridge and caricatures
the ensuing and at times surprisingly monosyllabic Bloomsbury
gatherings. It alludes to his promiscuity when it sardonically
mocks him as 'the idol of Wilts & many ladies, too many to
name, too illustrious to specify, carried locks of his hair in
their reticules, hence his comparative epidermic depilation in
later life', or when he jumps to the rescue of his mistress Mary
Hutchinson who has fallen into 'Rodmell brooks'.

One of the landmark scenes in 'The Messiah' is Clive's
meeting of the two Stephen sisters, Vanessa and Virginia,
whom he boldly confronts with a volume of Keats, and which,
as the narrative prophetically states, leads to 'the collision &

kaleidoscope of two shattered worlds'. 'The Messiah' presents Clive Bell as a combination of intellectual aesthete and boisterous country gentleman, and it parodies his aristocratic upbringing and his francophilia when it tells us that he is nearly taken for a descendant of 'the houses of Bourbon and Valois'. His passion for hunting is mocked in an episode when, during his agricultural work as a conscientious objector at Garsington Manor, the residence of the illustrious Lady Ottoline Morrell, Clive with a firm hand shoots Lady Ottoline's pet peacock.

The conflicts between life and art, and art as a way of life, form a central and recurring theme of most of the Supplements as they record the vagaries of the artists and their friends. The intense absorption of the artists in their work predictably leads to clashes between the artistic mind and their quotidian environment. Since the artistry of Charleston generates its own style of living, in which everyday life and objects were rigorously subordinated to art, these inevitably become a frequent target of irony. For instance, everyday objects like matchboxes lead to the exasperation of Clive Bell, who does not find any place for them in his aesthetically refined household at 46 Gordon Square.[21]

Like Clive Bell, Duncan Grant also strikes a comic figure when he is cast into the role of a prophet and saint who walks the streets of Bloomsbury in a blanket and is shipwrecked, as the text informs us, in the same spot as St. Paul. 'The Dunciad', written in 1924/1925, derives many of its satirical features from Pope. It portrays Duncan Grant's 'doubtful' birth, an event about which he himself is unsure, his unruly fearlessness as a child when he tries to kill another Anglo-Indian child, or when he presents a carrot to Queen Victoria. 'The Dunciad' exhibits Duncan Grant's extraordinary charm along with his clumsiness and dislike of public speeches. When at Charleston, where he feels much more at ease, he observes fantastical phenomena like a dancing fox, or, in an attempt to kill the weeds, sets the pond on fire and kills the fish instead. His many eccentricities include his somewhat rustic appearance at one of Lady Cunard's dinner parties where footmen have to remove straw and mice from his attire, and his Sisyphean attempts to reach spiritual illumination: 'Climbs Mt Serrat with Nessa: A second attempt to reach God. But he only found Nessa, Roger & two donkeys at the top. Accept no substitutes'. Like Vanessa Bell, he becomes famous for his neglect of the laws of nature, but bears all the ensuing mishaps with stoic equanimity.

Duncan Grant, Vanessa and Clive Bell prominently figure in 'Eminent Charlestonians', which was composed in 1923 and echoes Lytton Strachey's satirical portraits in *Eminent Victorians*. 'Eminent Charlestonians' contains short scenes about the adventures and carryings-on of many of the Charleston residents including the donkey Jesebel and the dog Henry. Chief among the dramatis personae of 'Eminent Charlestonians' are Nicholas and Barbara Bagenal, who experience the drawbacks of outdoor life when camping in the field near Charleston, and the servants Trissy and Emily. 'Eminent Charlestonians' renders episodes such as Trissy's persistent but unsuccessful pancake making and Emily's constant bad luck with handling china. It recalls their failed elopements and the notorious misfortunes of Alice the maid, who needs to be rescued on her hikes and is haunted by exploding squids.

Managing day-to-day life was not only challenging for the servants, but also for the artists. 'The Life and Death History of a Studio' from 1923/1924 is about building a new studio at Charleston and it mockingly contrasts the artists' high ambitions with their inability to put them into practice. While the other artists unsuccessfully contemplate the design of the studio, Vanessa Bell stands aloof from the undertaking, and escapes into the world of her imagination, where she is 'caught contemplating

Family and friends of Vanessa Bell at Charleston

by a Camel'. The first part of the story covers Duncan Grant's doomed attempt to build the studio, and the second part treats the arrival of Roger Fry, which initially promises help and success. However, despite Fry's enthusiasm, which is well-founded on theoretical knowledge, and fuelled by Ruskin's 'Seven lamps of architecture', the studio collapses twice, once over a cow that 'becomes a martyr for her zeal for art', and a second time it leaves the artists trapped in concrete in 'a scene of woe'.

The last of the illustrated Supplements, the 'Monthly Calendar' of 1927, contains illustrations of cars and planes in black ink and provides brief accounts of scattered events that took place in each month of the year. It is primarily concerned with Vanessa Bell's renting a cottage in the South of France, 'a land where there is no conversation, no society, no literature; where the inhabitants are dumb; where the sun always shines from the North; & the old & clear light untainted by intellect & undisturbed by passion which is necessary for the composition of still lives, perpetually prevails.' The entries for spring and summer tell about how Duncan Grant becomes a favourite among the local ladies of Cassis, and how a great rivalry develops between the 'Woolves's' car, a Singer, and the Bells' Renault. In its reminiscences of the autumn and winter months it returns to Charleston and its surroundings as it describes Tilton and the Keynes' parsimonious ways of entertaining guests at dinner.

As much as the Supplements are about the Charleston residents and visitors and about well-known Bloomsbury figures and their circles they are also about Charleston, the very place itself. Charleston not only emerges as the background to many of the adventures recorded, but as a creative space, a site of pleasures, games and fantasies and a refuge that stimulates the imagination. The Supplements therefore also treat the house and its rooms which, like the kitchen, become associated with particular incidents such as pancake making and the visit of a cow. They are about the garden, its weeds and the drastic but inefficient attempts to eradicate them, and they focus on the pond as a major scene of aquatic adventures, battles, attempts at landscape and water engineering, or pyrotechnical experiments. The household animals play vital parts and so do the cows in the adjacent fields, which Duncan Grant never failed to amaze, as in his display of Catherine wheels in the punt.

The pond at Charleston, like the lily pool in Virginia Woolf's last novel *Between the Acts*, is home to the carp, eels and to the ubiquitous mud that was of great interest to Quentin's pottery. At the end of *Between the Acts*, the mud, a metaphor for the artist's creative powers, becomes fertile as wonderful words rise from it. It might be this fertile mud of the imagination that *Between the Acts* resonates with so strongly, which had earlier inspired Virginia Woolf and Quentin Bell's collaborative adventures in the *Charleston Bulletin* Supplements.

CLAUDIA OLK

The Charleston Bulletin Supplements

The manuscripts of the *Charleston Bulletin* and the *Charleston Bulletin* Supplements belong to the British Library.

This is the first edition of the text of the Supplements to the *Charleston Bulletin*. The child Quentin Bell's spelling, punctuation and grammatical mistakes are reproduced as in the original manuscripts. The transcript has also retained Virginia Woolf's sometimes idiosyncratic spelling and punctuation. Unless otherwise indicated [*by the use of editorial square brackets*] all emphases, ellipses etc. are in the original texts.

Special Suplement
Xmas Number

CONTENTS

Special suplement. Xmas number. Charleston bulletin'; [1923]. Colophon: 'Published at the Hogarth Press, written by Virginia Wolf'. A life of Vanessa Bell dictated by Virginia Woolf, pictures and spelling by Quentin Bell. About 1000 words. 23 pages. 270 × 218 mm. BL Add. 83322.

SPECIAL SUPLEMENT

(1923)

XMAS
NUMBER

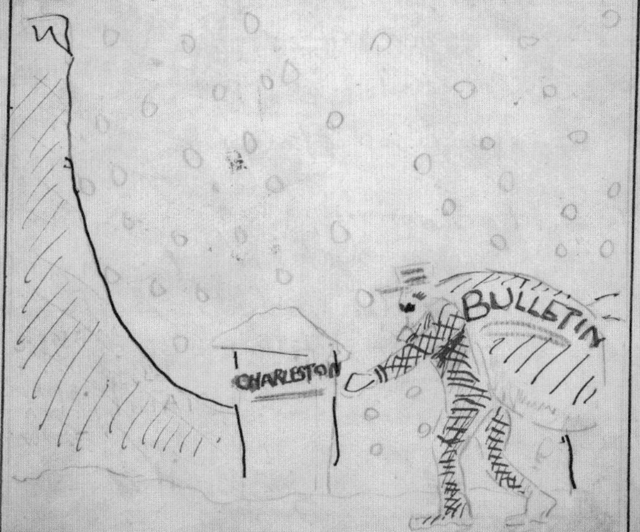

Scene no I in the Life of Mrs Bell

She ate her red beads.

In mistake for her porridge

Old nurse Lugton though

violent was too late.
Nessa ate six.

Scene 3

Her first and last catch
consisting of 150 chad these
being very retentife of life

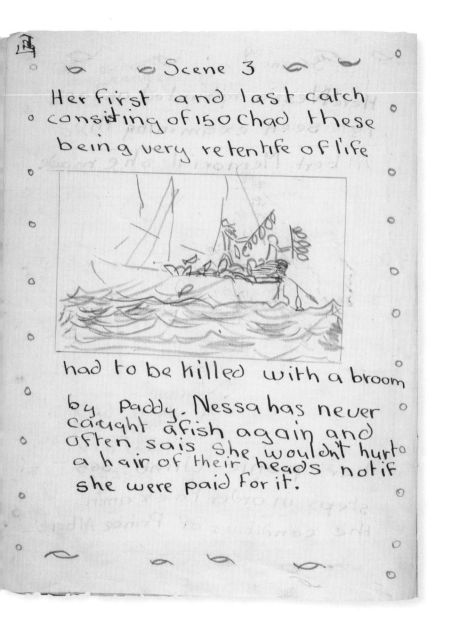

had to be killed with a broom
by paddy. Nessa has never
caught a fish again and
often sais she wouldnt hurt
a hair of their heads notif
she were paid for it.

Scene,
This prickly bush grew on the
loggan rock inspired by the
taunts of her juniors Nessa
determined to see for herself

wether her lost umbrella was on top
she climbed persistently for 6 hourse
and had to be rescued by proffessor Wolstenholme with a step ladder.

Scene no 1 in the Life of Mrs Bell

She ate her redbeads in mistake for her porridge
Old nurse Lugton[1] though violent was too late.
Nessa ate six.

Scene 2

Here Nessa mounted on Topsy is seen examining the Albert
Memorial she made her ponie climb 365 steps in order to
examin the condition of Prince Albert.

Scene 3

Her first and last catch consisting of 150 chad these being very
retentife of life had to be killed with a broom by Paddy. Nessa
has never caught a fish again and often sais she wouldn't hurt
a hair of their heads not if she were paid for it.

Scene 4

This pricklybush grew on the loggan rock[2] inspired by the
taunts of her Juniors Nessa determined to see for herself
wether her lost umbrella[3] was on top she climbed persistently
for 6 hours and had to be rescued by proffessor
Wolstenholme with a step ladder.[4]

Scene 5

Having spent 87£ 10s 6¾d on her bridesmaids dress silk
stockings and nightgoun for lady Magerites[5] wedding Nessa
and Adrian left the whole bundle in the 3rd class lavatory at
Swindon the rage and despair of Gorge Ducworth[6] the bridgroom is depicted.

Scene 6

The wedding day lady Magaret advances up the aisle from
which old Mrs Fisher[7] has been removed by an usher owing
to her widows dress which is thought ominous for the bride.

Scene 5

Having spent 87 £ 10.6.¾ on
her bridesmaids dress, silk
stockings and nightgown for
lady Magerites wedding

Nessa and Adrian left
the whole bundle in
the 3rd class lavatory
at Swindon the rage
and despair of Corge
Ducworth the bridgroom is
depicted.

The wedding day lady Mag
aret advances up the aisle

from which old Mrs
Fisher has been

removed by an usher owing
to her widows dress
which is thought ominous
for the bride.

Scene 8

This scene had better be
imagined than described
it is enough to say that the
article was white with

a greek key pattern
in orange.

Scene 9

Decipts the celebrated authoress
Mrs Humphry Ward ynderth
Arc de Triomphe attemphing
to invite Nessa to tea

dinner or lunch. All refused.

Scene 7

Nessas wedding day which began in the worst possible way because Sam the chauffer was a hypocritical snearing leering dastardly beast and lost his way like a needle in a camels eye as Nessa said whe she got to Padington an hour and a half late[8] but it's an ill wind that blows nobody any good[9] and it never rains but it pours. so saying she got into the train and was carried to Manorbia[10] where the honeymoon was spent in complete darkness.

Scene 8

This scene had better be imagined than described it is enough to say that the article was white with a greek key pattern in orange.[11]

Scen 9

Decipts the celebrated authoress Mrs. Humphry Ward[12] under th Arc de Triomphe attempting to invite Nessa to tea dinner or lunch. All refused.

Scene 9

An unfortunate incident at Fritham. surveying the bees with the post-master general one of the insects had the temerity to enter the drum of Nessa's ear and there kicked up such a racket that she said it was like twelve brass bands in a teapot. Austen Chamberlain[13] extracted the bee with a buttonhook.

Scene 10

Heris Nessa washing her hands in a Turkish well and seein if her ring will float they do not

Scene 9

An unfortunate incident at Fritham.

surveying the bees with
the post-master general
one of the insects had the

temerity to enter the drum of
Nessa's ear and there kicked
up such a racket that she
said it was like twelve
brass bands in a teapot.
Austen Chamberlain extracted the
bee with a buttonhook.

Scene 10

Heri's Nessa, washing her
hands in a turkish well
and seein if her ring

will Float they do not

SCENE 11

Now said Nessa I shall be very tactfull.

I shall write to poor Sylvia[14] and say thers no breaking bad news all your pictures have been refused. that's what I call tact in extremis said Nessa but no one else.

SCENE 12

Old madam No-non[15] was about to sit down. Non-non said the wicked imps Vanessa and Toby pulling the chair from under her she did not see the joke but fetched the master.

SCENE 13

Lawkamussy how them turkey do roam said Nessa why I declare whole pack of fowls flying to roost. but it was only on wren and two cock sparows.

SCENE 14

Have you no clothes to declare Madame? said the douanier No cigars pianos or scent. I have thre dozen trunks of china said Nessa I've lost everything else

SCENE 15

I thought a return ticket meant that one had to return the same way not the same day said Nessa but of course it did not so they had to pay twice over.

SCENE 16

Its an odd hour to start 3 in the morning said Nessa After waiting 8 hours they found it was the afternoon but did on this occasion catch the train.

Scene 14

Have you no clothes to declare
Madame? said the douanier
No cigars pianos or scent." I

NOWERVOZ|A ESPESCIALOVIA

have thredozen trunks of
china said Nessa lue lost
everythingelse

Scene 5

I thought a return ticket
meant that one had to return
the same way not the same
day said Nessa but o fcause

It did not so they had
to pay twice over.

SCENE 17

Hup hup cried Nessa as her ass climbed mounted Serrat to look for her lost umbrella it is a long lane that has no turning; A miss is as good as a mile larg motor car shaved off her donkeys whiskers.

SCENE 18

Well said Duncan, if that clock has been an hour Fast or 2 slow we might quite well have been in the train by now. Its a mere matter of time said Nessa.

SCENE 19

Thats the tenth pair of specs Ive' lost this week said Nessa I really believe the daws steal them & line their nests. Six pairs were found later firmly imbedded in her hair.

SCENE 20

Please do not touch, Nessa wrote 20 years ago in a plate of eggs. No one touched till Wednesday last no one ever wish to touch them again this contcludes for the present the marvellous adventures of Vanessa Bell, and a merry Christ mas and a Happy Newyear too.

THE END
PUBLISHED BY THE HOGARTH PRESS
written by Virginia Wolf

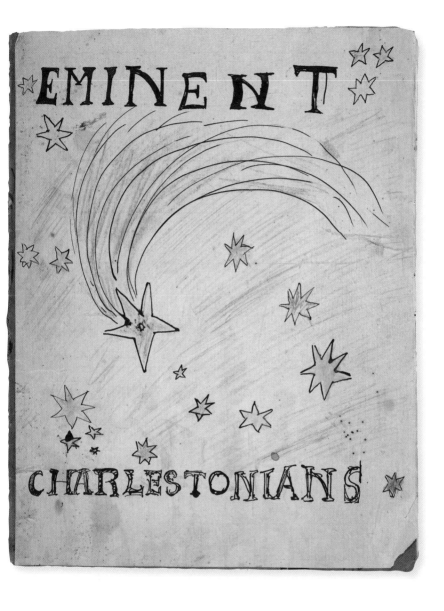

EMINENT

CHARLESTONIANS

Eminent Charlestonians

An Entirly original work
being 40 incidents described and illustrated
concerning 7 eminent Charlestonians

Contents

Charleston Bulletin. Vol. viii. 'Eminent Charlestonians: an entirely original work being 40 incidents described and illustrated concerning 7 eminent Charlestonians, by Mrs V Woolf & Q Bell'; [1923?]. With the imprint: 'Published by the Charleston Bulletin Press'. The text by and in the hand of Virginia Woolf and the illustrations and their captions by and in the hand of Quentin Bell. 273 × 215 mm. BL Add. 83323

Nena to save time, which she said, is a stitch in nine bought a bicycle, or some machine once Employed in carting corn, costing 2. 11. 3¾ & rode to Ashcham: but was forced by six large Dandelions to give up the perilous enterprise, having the

THE BLUE BOTTLE DANGER

Here Mr. Bell is seen Explaining how "them blue bottles do bottle, to be sure".

When eighteen large bombs fell upon Eastbourne, destroying the gasometer, the Church, & an entire row of bathing machines.

Chapter I: Nessa

Jesebel

Mrs. Bell leading home Jesebel, the donkey, which being incompetent to run, stand, or even make cats meat of. She paid £5.10.6 for; only to discover it fundamentally sour, passionate and vicious hearted. Death soon came; from a German bomb.

Bees

Nessa bought twenty patent bee hive fasteners at a Bazaar for the benefit of soldiers' widows. Insolent behaviour of bees. Exasperation of Nessa.

A stich in time

Nessa to save time, which she said, is a stitch in nine, bought a bicycle or some machine once employed in carting corn, costing 2.11.3¾ & rode to Asheham: but was forced by six large dandelions to give up the perilous enterprise. having the

The blue bottle danger

Here Mrs. Bell is seen explaining how "them blue bottles do bottle to be sure." When eighteen large bombs fell upon Eastbourne, destroying the gasometer, the church, & an entire row of bathing machines.

Chap II Clive

Clive and the concertina

Mr. Bell mistaking a concertina for a cat: or a cat for a concertina; nobody can say which, since the creature gave a scritch & nothing remained but a horrid stinking, steaming, puss of pitch.

CLIVE AND THE CONCERTINA

Mr Bell mistaking a Concertina for a Cat; or a Cat for a concertina; nobody can say which, since the Creature gave a Scritch, & nothing remained but a horrid, stinking, steaming, "puss" of pitch.

RESCUE ~~MISS~~ MARY.

Sudden disappearance of Mr St John Hutchinson in Rodmell Brooks.

Mr Bell is here seen saving what remained: two feet, one hand, 3 inches of pink drawers, & a copy of the 'Holy Bible, which Wm H: had stolen from Leonard Woolf, Esquire.

When we
consider the
baldness of
Clive Bell,
we are
all tempted
to ascribe
it to the
indiscriminate
application
of fresh
snow balls
to an
insufficiently
protected
pate.

Or, we
may hazard
the assumption
that the
said
depilation
of the scalp
supervened
upon the
discovery
of the
infestation
by
Lepidoptera
of his second
best suit
of evening
clothes.

3

1) POSSIBLE Reason why Clive lacks hair

4

2) Possible Reason why Clive lacks hair

2 Rescues Mary

Sudden disappearance of Mrs. St John Hutchinson[16] in Rodmell Brooks. Mr. Bell is here seen saving what remained: two feet, one hand, 3 inches of pink drawers, & a copy of the Holy Bible, which Mrs. H. had stolen from Leonard Woolf, Esquire.

3 1) Possible Reason why Clive lacks hair

When we consider the baldness of Clive Bell, we are tempted to ascribe it to the indiscriminate application of fresh snow balls to an insufficiently protected pate.

4 2) Possible Reason why Clive lacks hair

Or we may hazard the assumption that the said depilation of the scalp supervened upon the discovery of the infestation by lepidoptera of his second best suit of evening clothes.

5 His prowess

It is understood that Clive Bell Esquire attained his present undisputed eminence in the world of Art & Letters by his skill in the science of equitation, & his vulpine ascendancy, here displayed to which his Literary zeal, & familiarity with the Classics of our tongue, here displayed, added little or nothing of ponderable gravity.

6 7 The chocolates

Mr. Bell yielding to his passion for sweetmeats. A box at a time is the only rhyme, he said & poor Quentin went hungry to bed.

8 Rewards of virtue

Here we have depicted the celebrated scene, when through a singular natural similarity of countenance, the well-known M.P. Churchill received the tribute designed for Bell the critic.[17]

HIS PROWESS

It is understood
that Clive Bell
Esquire
attained his
present undisputed
eminence in the
world of Art &
Letters by
his skill in the
hiena of
Equitation, this
vulpine
as tendency
here
displayed

6

due to which is
this Literary
Zeal, &
familiarity with
the Classics of
our tongue
here displayed,
but added
little or nothing
of ponderable
Gravity & the
his rage have
largely if not
entirely added
when

Mr. Bell
yielding to
his
passion
for
sweetmeats.
A box at
a time;
is the only
rhyme,
he said, &
poor Quentin
went
hungry to
bed.

Here we
have depicted
the the celebrated
scene, when
through a
singular
natural
similarity
of countenance,
the well known
M.P. Churchill
carved the
statute
designed for
Bell the
Critic.

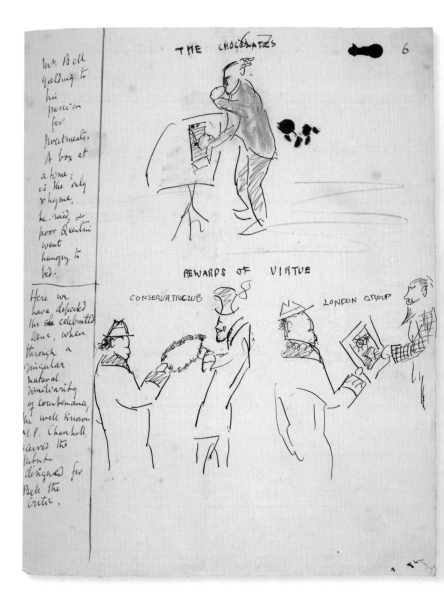

THE CHOCOLATES

REWARDS OF VIRTUE

CONSERVATIVE CLUB

LONDON GROUP

I Duncan

1 Duncan determined to show the cows some of the delights of life, went on board the punt & set fire to 18 Catherine wheels, which lit up the horizon for many miles, & tore several large holes in his trousers.

2 A fellow artist studying water effects with Duncan Grant as a model.

3 Duncan rescuing a child, at enormous risk to Sir Leslie Stephen's grey tweed suit.

4 Inspired by their love of art, Mr. Fry & Mr. Grant roped themselves together & suffered acutely from vertigo on a pediment or gargoyle or waterspout or gothic erection on Salisbury Cathedral.

5 A simple episode: verdiquisation of Grant.

6 Another Simple Episode connected with the return from Rangoon. A solitary spinster is observed afloat in a boat. A whale approaches. She has little chance of life.

What escaped from Duncans Hair

What escaped was long and oily & slimy; dark & thin & liquescent; reddish blueish, greenish: it had rings, no head, & no legs, it slithered & whirled; it ate cabbage; it was in short no more & no less than one of natures most repulsive pests, the inhabitant of garden beds (where its office is said to be benign) but the table is turned when it takes to inhabiting the heads of gentlemen at table; as in this case it did, falling therefrom to the salad mayonnaise & causing Harland,[18] very naturally & rightly, one of the most painful emotions of a life which has not been entirely free from sorrow: it was, in short, A WORM.

Duncan determined to show the farm yard cows some of the delights of life, went on board the punt, & set fire to 18 Catherine wheels, which lit up the horizon for many miles, & tore several large holes in his trousers.

A fellow artist studying water effects with Duncan Grant as model.

I

2

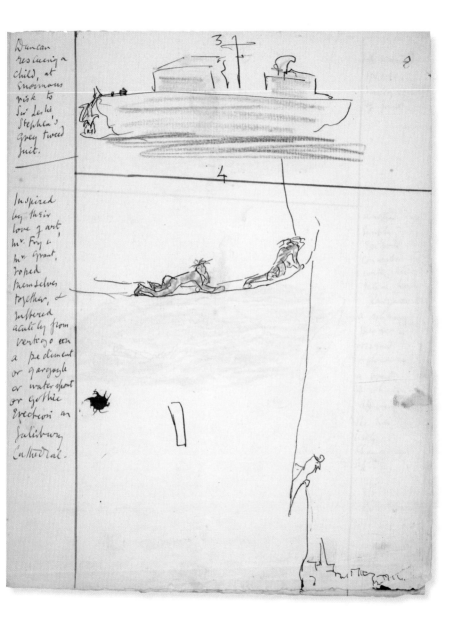

Duncan
rescuing a
child, at
enormous
risk to
Sir Leslie
Stephen's
grey tweed
suit.

Inspired
by their
love of art
Mr. Fry &
Mr. Grant,
roped
themselves
together, &
suffered
acutely from
vertigo on
a pediment
or gargoyle
or waterspout
or gothic
erection on
Salisbury
Cathedral.

3

4

8

5

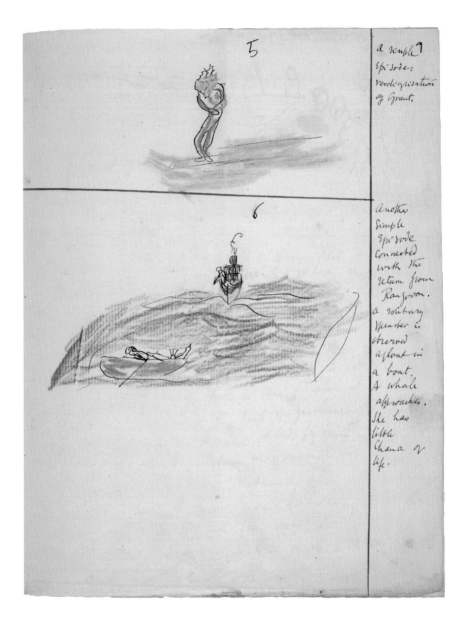

6

The Bagnells

1 Simple lifing

A young couple called Hiles & Bagenal[19] slept out in a field to save house rent. God, who saw through this sent a bolt & a large branch to warn them & so Mr Bell had to open the house at dead of night, very furious, in a black rage.

2 Mr Bacnal overcome

Next day, rather weakened, Mr. Bagenal was overcome by gas fumes in a haystack

Trisy[20]

1 Pancake day

When in a good & merry mood, Trisy would seize a dozen eggs & a bucket of flour, coerce a cow to milk itself, & then mixing the ingredients toss them 20 times high up over the skyline, & catch them as they fell in dozens & dozens & dozens of pancakes.

2 Trisys porridge

But her porridge was a very different affair. This was costive close & crusty. It dolloped out of a black pan in lumps of mortar. It stank; it stuck.

3 Trisy meets royalty

This represents the physical prostration of Trisy Stacey at the prospect in the far future of being possibly allowed to break bread at the same table or under the same awning with George Edward Albert Cecil Henry James Stuart Windsor Plantagenet Prince of Wales.

THE BAGNELLS
1 SIMPLE LIFING

A young
Couple
Called Hiles
& Bagenal
slept
out in
a

field to
save house
rent. God,
who saw
through them,
sent a bolt &
a large branch
to warn them
& so Mrs
Bell had to
open the
house
at dead of
night, very
furious, in
a black rage.

Neg day,
rather
weakened
Mr
Bagenal
was over
come by
Gas
fumes
in a
hay stack.

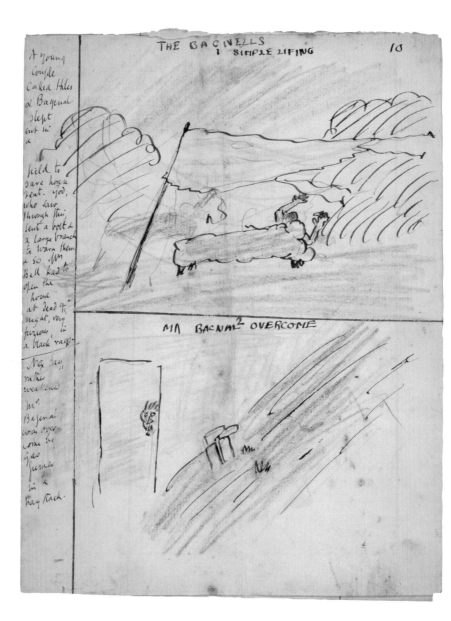

MR BAGNAL 2 OVERCOME

When in a good
& merry mood
Trisy would
seize a dozen
eggs & a bucket
of flour, coerce a
cow to milk itself,
& then mixing
the ingredients
toss them 20
times high up over
the skyline, &
catch them as
they fell in dozens
& dozens &
dozens of pancakes

But her porridge was
a very different affair.
This was costive
close & crusty.
It dolloped out of a
black pan in
lumps of mortar.
It stank. it
stuck.

TRISY
1
PANCAKE DAY

TRISYS PORRIDGE
2

3
TRIXY MEETS ROYALTY

4
AN ASSININE ACT

This represents the
physical prostration
of Trixy Stacey at
the prospect in the
far future of being
possibly allowed
to break bread
at the same table
on with the same
awning with
George Edward Albert
Cecil Henry James
Stuart Windsor
Plantagenet Prince
of Wales.

Still disordered by
the said prospect
of Royalty, she
have legged to the
Red Cross, thus
ensuring its
speedy disruption.

4 An assinine act

Still disordered by the said prospect of Royalty, she gave
Jezebel to the Red Cross; thus ensuring its speedy disruption.

5 Henry and the pancake

Tossing the pancake over the beech bough it broke on Henry's
head, forming a fine natural collar, of strength durability &
power to resist damp.

6 Trissy and Gerald

It was while shooting a Duck that Gerald Stacey won Trisies
heart.

Emily[21]

1 Emily at work

Little is needed to illustrate this forcible scene: at her best she
could destroy 40 pieces of china in one minute

2 Emily at play

When resting, she attended to the lighter crocks – such as
tooth glasses, chamber pots, & old china generally.

3 Emily & Yak-i-Yak

This love episode was simple, but, while it lasted, strong.

4 An unsuccesful elopement

One fine night, the lovers escaped: but misjudging the gate,
the cart, the horse, the moon, the hour & everything, this
was the upshot cart here, man there, legs of woman there.

Little
is needed
to illustrate
this forcible
scene:
at her best,
she could
destroy 40
pieces of China
in one minute

When resting,
she attended
to the
lighter
crocks —
such as
fresh glazes,
chamber pots,
& old
China
generally.

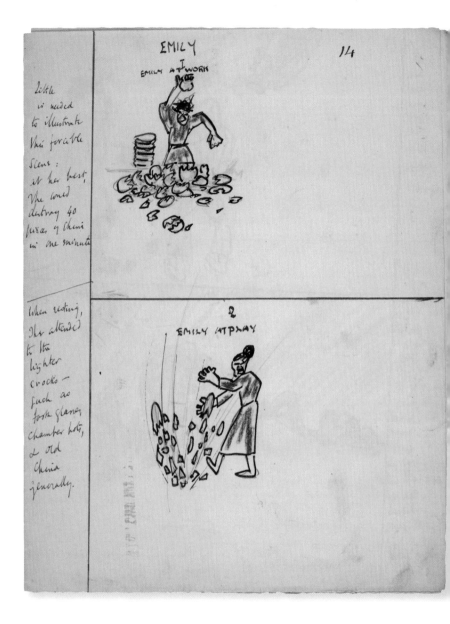

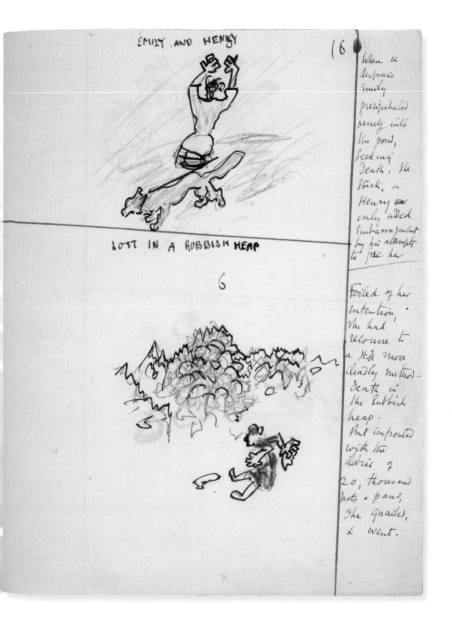

EMILY. AND HENRY

LOST IN A RUBBISH HEAP

6

When in despair Emily precipitated herself into the pond, seeking Death, the Stork. & Henry only added embarrassment by his attempts to free her

Foiled of her intention. she had recourse to a still more deadly method- Death in the Rubbish heap. But confronted with the debris of 20, thousand pots & pans, she quailed, & went.

Now plucking up heart, as death disowned her for his Bride, she took part in the Egg & Spoon celebrations & the great European war. So drastic was her foot, even now, that no Egg lived one second in her proximity.

Sometimes again in a wild despair she would engage the Bull in antics, of which this is no exaggerated representation.

7

THE EGG AND SPOON RACE !?

8

EMILY AND MR H EX'S BULL

5 Emily and Henry

When in despair Emily precipitated herself into the pond, seeking Death, she stuck so Henry only added embarrassment by his attempts to free her.

6 Lost in a rubbish heap

Foiled of her intention, she had recourse to a still more deadly method – death in the Rubbish heap. But confronted with the debris of 20 thousand pots & pans, she quailed & went.

7 The egg and spoon race

Now plucking up heart, as death disowned her for his Bride, she took part in the egg & spoon celebrations of the great European war. So drastic was her foot, even now, that no egg lived one second in her proximity

8 Emily and Mr Hex's bull[22]

Sometimes again,in a wild despair, she would engage the Bull in antics of which this is no exaggerated representation.

[The Upps]

1 Alice Arrives[23]

Miss A. succeded to the throne stepping from a fine milk cart, in a red dress, on a bright summer evening, when everything predicted peace.

2 Alice and Yak-i-Yak

And the first person who came her way was no less a character than Yaki-Yak, still lame, after his elopement but otherwise equipped for intercourse.

Alice Arrives

Alice and Yahi-Yak

Miss A.
Succeeded to
the throne
stepping from
a fine milk
cart, in a
red dress, in a
blight summer
evening, when
everything
predicted peace

And the first
person who
came her way
was no less
a character
than
Yaki-Yak.
Still came, after
his elopement
but otherwise
equipped for
intercourse.

Mrs. U— Goes to Eastbourne in a Pale pink Frock[24]

Determined to show the people of Eastbourne what she rightly thought they could not in their wildest dreams imagine – her new pink dress, with 7 flounces & primrose yellow parasol, Mrs. Up: took the pier by storm. There was frantic crying & much disorder.

Miss A— caught Napping

Nor were the dreams of Miss A. altogether blank of omen. Sleeping at her ease, suddenly she was lifted to the rafters, & violently concussed by a ham, through the explosion of a squid behind.

Meets cow in the kitchen

No sooner was she descended from these heights, than a cow, entering the kitchen, forced her to seek refuge on the table, where she embayed herself, poker in fist, bonnet pin in mouth.

Attempts to climb the Beacon

Judging herself insecure, & preferring nature to man, she clomb the Beacon; but was once more buffeted back by the ac- & declivities of that famous bulwark – in short, she stuck, and was only hauled down, at grave peril, by Lord Gage in person,[25] armed with a gun.

Takes Henry out for a walk

Still the lower animals remained & to Henry she turned for comfort, help & protection. Unfortunately the hare ran, the string broke and Miss A was again discomposed, this time in the mud.

determined to
show the people of
Eastbourne what
she nightly thought
they could not in
their wildest
dreams imagine—
her new pink silk,
with 7 flounces, &
primrose yellow
parasol. Mrs
Up: took the
pier by storm.
There was frantic
crying; & much
disorder.

Nor were the dreams
of Miss A:
altogether blank of
omen. Sleeping
at her ease, suddenly
she was lifted
to the rafters, &
violently concussed by
a ham, through
the explosion of a
squib behind.

Mrs O— Goes to Eastbourne in a
Pale pink Frock

Miss A— caught Napping

MEETS COW IN THE KITCHEN

ATTEMPTS TO CLIMB THE BEACON

No sooner after
She descended
from there
heights, than a
cow, entering
the kitchen
forced her to seek
refuge on the
table, where
she' embayed
herself, poker
in fist bonnet
him in mouth.

Judging herself
insecure, &
preferring nature
to man, she
climbt the
Beacon; but
was once more
buffeted back
by the ac- &
declivities of that
famous
'bulwark — in
short, she stuck,
& was only
hauled down, at
grave peril, by
Lord Yage in
person, armed with
a gun.

Writes to the Bulletin

Driven from pillar to post, with no refuge in roost, she applied herself, as a final resort to pen and ink and produced in the space of 5 hours, 6 lines of reading matter of an obscene contentious inflammatory & libellous nature, which would have continued indefinitely had the ink pot not soaked through on to Mr Keynes bald head.

THE END

THE LIFE AND DEATH
HISTORY OF A STUDIO

HERE LIES
COW
SUSAN
OBIT
JUNE 1929

BY VIRGINIA WOOLF

The Life and Death History of a Studio

Contents

1 Mrs. Bell caught contemplating by a Camel

Mrs. Bell while contemplating the studio in Fitzroy Street was struck by the hot breath of a Camel. Mistrusting the Eastern Beast she fled into the area of a Boarding house, where she contemplated undisturbed, the camel meanwhile devouring six dogs, half a cat, & a barrel of beer.

'The life and death history of a studio. By Virginia Woolf'; [1924?]. The text is by and in the hand of Virginia Woolf and the illustrations and their captions by and in the hand of Quentin Bell. On the building of a new studio at Charleston. About 800 words. 12 pages. 283 × 220 mm. BL Add. 83324.

2 DUNCAN GETS (SOME?) DISTEMPER

The camel disposed of, Duncan set out to procure distemper, which by malfeasance, he mistook for a disorder affecting unweaned dogs, cats, mammals, rodents & all beasts above the rank of the sea anemone, as he explained to the chemist, who referred him to Windsor & Newton's colour shop,[26] interpreting his symptoms correctly as those of a famous painter: 12lbs. of Chinese white was delivered.

3 COLLECTING IMPEDIMENTA

The great collection of commodities for making the studio now began: consisting of drain pipes, old hats, 25 vols. on architecture, sheeps jaw bones, walking sticks, enamel bed pans, water troughs, tooth brushes, fenders, chalk, cheese, mousetraps & glass tumblers: Duncan is shown beneath.

4 PLANNING THE STUDIO

Four experts exhibit their behind views, their fronts being entirely absorbed by the mental strain of combining Gothic, Runic, Corinthian and Palladian (or Pompeian) architectural styles in the studio.

Beneath, an assortment of theodolites & telescopes, plumb leads, surveying telescopes, spirit levels, ball bearing oil finders & compasses which may come in handy.

5 MR ROGER FRY ARRIVES

Mr Fry arrives to rebuild studio with his own hands: 25 tons of concrete; the help of Mr Ruskin's 7 lamps of architecture;[27] & his own formidable, gristly, grumpy, grousely, ill-temper (Hah!hah!) combined with Quaker instincts.

III

Collecting impedimenta

The first great collection of commodities for making the
studio now began: Consisting of drain pipes, nk hats, 25 vols. on architecture,
sheeps jaw bones, walking sticks, enamel bed pans,
water troughs, tooth brushes, fenders, chalk, cheese,
mousetraps, & glass tumblers: Duncan is thrown
beneath.

Four experts Exhibit their behind views, their fronts
being entirely absorbed by the mental strain
of combining Gothic, Renaissance, Corinthian,
& Palladian (or Pompeian) architectural
Styles in the Studio.

Beneath, an assortment of theodolites &
telescopes, plumb leads, surveying telescopes,
mirror levels, ball bearing oil finders &
compasses which may come in handy.

FINAL DEMOLITION OF OLD STUDIO

On arrival a gigantic gush was heard; a Stink was
Stunk: to wit, one cow, 17 melons, 184 apples, 6
b-irds (species unknown) all decomposing & exploding & driving the old
Studio to its demolition against the setting sun,
in the midst of which Duncan's legs may be
Seen, & Mr. Bell Expostulating.

6 Final demolition of old studio

On arrival a gigantic gush was heard; a stink was stunk: to wit, one cow, 17 melons, 184 apples, 6 birds (species unknown) all decomposing & exploding & driving the old studio to its demolition against the setting sun, in the midst of which Duncan's legs may be seen & Mrs. Bell expostulating.

7 Discovery of a dead cow

Duncan recognising an old, if fiery friend, in the horns which protrude from the ashes, affixed a rope & drew to the surface the bloated corpse of his friend, Cow Susan, now unfortunately a martyr to her zeal for art, in search of which she had visited the studio 2 years previous, & died of the fright in the wainscot.

8 Contemplation of ruins

Mr. Grant & Mrs. Bell contemplating the ruins of the studio; tears drop on the hissing ashes; the bones of the cow alone remain to mark the grave of so much – stink.

9 Duncan flings out a beam

Duncan makes projection on approved principles. Destruction of roof ensues & exodus of wasps & hornets to take up quarters in goats beards.

10 Aerial Survey

Mr. Fry (it is thought) contemplating heavens with a view to improvements.

Meeting of artists Mr. Roger Fry in the chair

Mr. Roger Fry remarking to Mr. Grant and Mrs. Bell how easily he would rebuild the studio if he were allowed to experiment on his own account: replies unprintable, manure arrives; also bullocks hair & concrete in tubs; Roger gets up

DISCOVERY OF A DEAD COW.

Duncan recognising an old, if feery friend, in the
horns which protrude from the ashes, affixed a
rope & drew to the surface the bloated corpse
of his friend, Cow Susan, now unfortunately
a martyr to her zeal for art, in search of
which she had visited the studio 2 years previous,
& died of the fright in the wainscot.

CONTEMPLATION OF RUINS

Mr. Grant & Mrs. Bell contemplating the ruins of
the studio; ~~from~~ tears drop on the hissing ashes;
the bones of the cow alone remain to mark
the grave of so much — stük.

THE ARTISTS // INCARCERATED

This is the last scene, which shows the artists
fixed in the concrete: M.ʳ William Ford falling from the roof
Clive Bell pronouncing his final denunciation of the whole
asinine undertaking & night descending on a scene of woe.

early; charters two farm horses; & begins by tunnelling beneath the kitchen, thus bringing down Mrs. Uppington,[28] & 25 male rats: 2 tons of plaster; Mr. Upp's false teeth; ceiling beam; birds nests; eggs whisks; etc; etc; not greatly to his dismay, but upsetting to domestic life in a small scale, so that Mrs. Upp: left in a huff.

11 THE ARTISTS INCARCERATED

This is the last scene, which shows the artists fixed in the concrete; Mr. William Ford[29] falling from the roof, Clive Bell pronouncing his final denunciation of the whole asinine undertaking; & night descending on a scene of woe.

The Dunciad

Contents

'The Dunciad' by Virginia Woolf, illustrated by Quentin Bell; [the date 1924 is marked in pencil on top of the page]. With the imprint: 'The New Bulletin Publishing Co (Xmas season)'. A satire on Duncan Grant, with text by and in the hand of Virginia Woolf and the illustrations and their captions as well as the contents and chapter headings are by and in the hand of Quentin Bell. About 1200 words. 12 pages. 415 × 268 mm. BL Add 83326.

THE.DUNCIAD

BY VIRGINIA WOOLF

THE NEW BULLETIN PUBLISHING C

(XMAS SEASON)

18   climbs Cathedral

19   paints melon

20   climbs mt. Serrat (with nessa)

21   makes speech

THE DUNCIAD[30]
CONCERNING DUNCAN GRANT

1 BIRTH (DOUBTFUL)

Date of birth c. 1870–1880–1890
Several professors are at this moment industriously engaged in
synchronising the birth with the sun as it touches the
Pilgrims Stone at Stonehenge, what is supposed to settle the
matter. Mrs. Grant, however, says it happened on Friday,
between dinner & going to bed. Duncan is not sure that it
ever happened at all.

2 TRIES TO KILL SMALL CHILD

When Duncan was even younger than he is now, he came
possessed of a biscuit tin with which he attempted to murder
another Anglo-Indian child. Unfortunately he failed, as Mrs.
Grant rushed to the rescue. He was not punished, for he was
always a spoilt child.

3 CLIMBS PAGODA

Cf. Nessa on Holly tree (Life and adventures of Mrs. Bell,
p. 36).

4 FALLS OFF TOPDECK

The first and original crack occurred, it is thought, when he
fell in pursuit of a red ball from the deck & sustained fracture
of the jaw bone & head piece never securely mended since.

5 SHIPWRECK

Cf: St. Paul. For the benefit of our unbaptised readers we may say that St Paul was shipwrecked off Malta on his way to Rome to convert the Romans. Now history repeats itself! Duncan Grant came from Rangoon in the Marie Celeste[31] to convert the people of Bloomsbury to walking the streets in a blanket.[32] He was wrecked in the identical spot with St Paul, but no trace of the earlier prophet was found.

6 KISSED BY VICTORIA

Rothiemurchus,[33] 1886. Her majesty was opening a fountain in honour of the Prince Consort when Duncan Grant stepped forward & offered a nosegay of carrots & beans, picked by himself in the back garden attached to the burial ground of the Grants for 10 centuries. Queen Victoria never having seen a carrot naked, thought very highly of the sweet little boy, & gave him a cairngorm[34] from her bosom, which he sucked thinking it a sweet, & had therefore instantly & without ceremony, other than hand wiping by a napkin, to be removed.

7 TAKEN TO BEDLAM

(But uncle Trevor is now in Bed.)[35]

8 RESCUES CHILD

From Barge Aholibah on Cam. in Sir Leslie's trousers, now used for dress purposes only.[36]

9 THE FATE OF DUNCANS COATS

And Sir Leslies Waterloo Paddington Gare St Lazare, Liverpool Street Euston, Kings X, Victoria, St Pancras, Cannon Street, Charing Cross, Gard du Nord, Gare du Lyon, Marylebone, Lewes, Baker Street etc, etc, etc, etc.

7
Taken to Bedlam

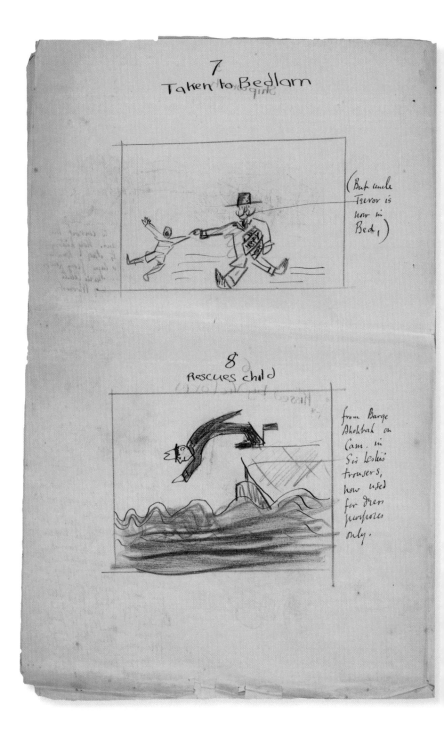

(But uncle
Trevor is
now in
Bed.)

8
Rescues child

from Barge
Aholibah on
Cam. in
Sir Leslie's
trousers,
now used
for dress
purposes
only.

The Charleston
Rodeo.
(Please note
R.S.P.C.A.)

12
Steals Lemoncurd

The first act:
Sick next;
& next;
& next.
A curtain is
Drawn.
Finis.

10 Dines in Whitehall

First visit to Lady Cunard.[37] This great patroness of the arts requiring decorations in her bathroom sent for Grant who arrived from the country having lately rolled to scratch himself in a Barn. Consequently the footmen were busy picking out straws, dandelions, small field mice, rats eggs, clouded yellow butterflies, nettles, darnocks, fossils, & other small field objects, during luncheon. But Duncan was entirely unmoved & made the largest meal of his life, off gold plate.

11 Kills cow

The Charleston Rodeo (Please note R.S.P.C.A.)

12 Steals lemon curd

The first act: sick next; & next; & next. A curtain is drawn. Finis

13 Sees dancing fox

This thought better to leave the fox to dance in vacuum; as no authoritative account of this "romantic phenomenon" (to quote Julian Bell, Essay on the art of war, p. 6.) was ever credibly enunciated. Mushrooms have since been picked on the spot.

14 Sets fire to his pocket

The fire engine follows, but not in time to discredit the legend that Grant has a burning tail. This has done him much harm in polite circles, in conjunction with the episode of the rats eggs in the hair (v. Lady Cunard, Ritz Hotel).

15 Walks from Gordon to Fitzroy Square in a blanket

For a bet, which he won at the cost of what little reputation for chastity, sobriety, respectability, prudence, decency, cleanliness, humanity, orderly conduct, morality, Christianity, temperance, common sense, sanity & brotherly love he may have once been supposed by the benignant to possess.

16 CLIMBS CATHEDRAL

In order to get nearer to Heaven, he set off to climb to the top of Notre Dame on a Wednesday morning, but owing to the gargoyles catching his trousers & meeting a party of American Schoolmistresses in a state of comparative nudity, he was forced to hide behind a Devil, & there stopped for the present. God being beyond him.

N.B. his trousers were torn, not the American schoolmistresses.

17 PAINTS MELON

The family melon which was meant for Dinner was seized by Duncan & used as a still life at the end of six weeks it had liquefied owing to the action of bacteria, when an attempt was made to remove it it collapsed & rendered the room uninhabitable while we remained at St. Tropez, & Mrs. Bell was forced to pay Ron Vildrac[38] for the damage done by a decomposing melon.

18 CLIMBS MT SERRAT WITH NESSA

A second attempt to reach God. But he only found Nessa, Roger & two donkeys at the top. Accept no substitutes.

19TH AND LAST   MAKES SPEECH

Duncan Grant rose & said: ——— Ladies & Gentlemen, I have the pleasure of addressing er, er, er , – I am sure we are all very glad. Mr. Chairman, my friends, I think I have said quite enough, I am not a professional speaker, I am not feeling well, I hope you have all enjoyed yourselves it is a very fine night I wish you would not throw things at me, I will now

Makes speech

When can Grant rose & said:— Ladies & Gentlemen I have the pleasure of addressing' Et ste Etcetra,— I am sure we are all very glad— Mr Chairman, my friends, I think I have said quite enough, I am not a professional Speaker, I am not feeling well, I hope you have all enjoyed yourselves this a very fine night. I wish you would not throw things at me, I will now conclude, I am sure we all feel deeply to the services for Mr. Adenleys very good President,—I butter-cups? butter-cups?— We hope that we will never have a worse president than he was a praline. Amen." he fell to the green ground & was retired

A voice from the crowd says mn mn mn

Scene in St Pauls.

This occurred after a gigantic eating bout, when Turkeys, sausages, ham, pies, venison, toffee, tarts, cakes, sardines, jam, tinned salmon, apricots, eel pie, strawberry ice, lemonade, sirloin & beef & yorkshire pudding, bread pudding, & Chocolate were eaten to such an extent that Duncan had no room for the last Chocolate, which stuck out, as is shown in picture & was removed by Mr___. Miss Rose Paul the Matron between her fingers.

conclude, I am sure we all feel deeply to the services for Mr. Adeney[39] is very good President – A voice from the crowd says mm mm mm – buttercups ? – buttercups ? – We hope that we will never have a worse president than he was a painter. Amen. He fell to the ground and was retired.

Scene in St. Pauls

This occurred after a gigantic eating bout, when Turkeys, Sausages, ham, pies, venison, toffee, tarts, cakes, sardines, jam, tinned salmon, apricots, eel pie, strawberry ice, lemonade, sirloin of beef & Yorkshire pudding, bread pudding, & chocolate were eaten to such an extent that Duncan had no room for the last chocolate, which stuck out, as is shown in picture & was removed by Miss Rose Paul the Matron between her fingers.

Setting the Thames on Fire[40]

Wishing to get rid of the weeds & the remaining dead fish he stopped a charabanc & borrowed some petrol which he poured on the pond & set on fire. This destroyed the following fish:

758 minnows
29 roach
98 carp, of which 67 were dead before
3 trout
1 pike
1 anchovy
1 herring
1 sardine (only the tin was found)
3 porpoises
758 eels
3 flying fish
23 crabs

1 smallish whale

plants: 3 oaks

1 willow

5 bay bushes

1 holly with umbrella attached

grass. sedge. vetch. potatoes, carrots, rabbit food, etc. etc.

animals: 1 cow not mad

15 sheep

1 pig (small) 4 cats 12 rabbits 1 mouse

miscellaneous property – Mr. Ford's cup 1 grand piano, 1
Sewing machine 2 reapers for threshing machine.

NO WEED WAS DESTROYED!!!!!

AN ODORIFEROUS ACCIDENT

(For this vide correspondence in Charleston Bulletin.)
The carp in Charleston pond had died, come to the surface &
rotted. For no known reason Duncan wished to remove them,
He set out on the punt which was leaking & half full of water
& attempted to tow in the fish in a beehive. They were then
landed, placed in a wheelbarrow & they were taken into the
kitchen garden & buried. During the process the fish broke
into small pieces, & the smell was so fearful that all the
onlookers except Duncan were sick.

A LETTER TO THE NATION

This one of the most important documents for a full
understanding of the Dunciad was composed by D.G: posted,
sent & received at the Nation office where it put Old Mr.
Randall[41] in such a fury that he swallowed a small china
ornament & has made a whistling noise ever since. Mrs. Jones
was also incommoded; Mr. Henderson[42] came out in spots,
and Faulkner the office boy accidentally crashed a valuable
specimen of the pot makers art, such was his incredulous
despair. Note Date. [165th Nov. 1821]

2 Rothiemurcus Avenue

Dearest Sir

I plead to enclose submitted handscript when if per hazard
it mis liketh your prospectfull Editorship, which you will
drop into envelope on my escalated number heretofore
inscribed as above which I shall be sorry if it does,
Nevertheles al the same yours of the instantly obedient.
David Grant Gordon Square Duncan Grant of Bedlam
Bloomsbury, Charleston cum Tilton, neer Lewes, near near
but not very near Rodmell Sussex

165th Nov. 1821

This has more meanings than one and should be given careful
attention. It appears that Duncan Grant set out with the
intention of walking to France from Charleston but was
inconvenienced by the prevalence of somewhat uneven
ground in the neighbourhood of the Channel. Summoning
some fishermen by his cries, he was lowered on the end of a
string, many small objects such as letters, pictures, cutlery of
all kinds, one Belgian hare, & a thousand toothpicks being
lost in transit. He arrived at his destination quite unmoved, &
has continued the same ever since.

FINIS.

The Messiah

'The Messiah'; 1925. A satire on Clive Bell and other Bloomsbury celebrities, with text by and in the hand of Virginia Woolf and the illustrations and their captions by and in the hand of Quentin Bell. About 2000 words. 38 pages. 265 × 206 mm. BL Add. 83328.

THE MESSIAH

I

NATIVITY

1 "THE NATIVITY"

It was on a mild September morning in an old manorial Hall among horned cows, bisons, foxes, hunters & the feet of buffalo that our hero, the Messiah of Bloomsbury first screeched his first screech, wild, raucous, inspired, shrill. As is here depicted: but what his fury was thus early, whether an innate dislike of horns & hoofs, Bells & Bisons, cannot be stated. The doctor was puzzled.

2 THE FIRST MEET

At a very early age a red suit was bought for him to match his flaming yellow hair, at that time often compared to the sun sinking over the ocean bed, & he was set a-horse-back. He proved himself at once a Master of the Reins; to such an extent that, after out-galloping the hunt, led by the Duke of Beaufort,[43] he was tarred with foxes blood and given the Brush to hang up in his nursery. From that hour he was the idol of Wilts & many ladies, too many to name, too illustrious to specify, carried locks of his hair in their reticules, hence his comparative epidermic depilation in later life.

3 BEING BLOODED

The reader is requested to refer to page 2 for particulars of a scene which, though carefully concealed as the Messiah burgeoned, was yet at the foundation of much that will be manifest later: this is the Duke Blooding the Boy Bell.

4 FIRST ARTISTIC PROTEST

Like many other Christian households, that of the Bells expressed itself with energy & discrimination, bounty and chaste munificence in Christmas cards – such as roses, snow, churchyard scenes, robins, widows, frost etc: which, once displayed, were carefully nailed by old Nurse to the wall;

BEING BLOODED

ARRIVAL 5 AT CAMBRIDGE

accumulating in such conglomerations that little of the wall could be seen. So Clive, at the age of six, did a man's work. With his own hands he broke, battered, bruised & utterly bombarded the said cards, & gave vent, uproariously to his first recorded art criticism. Blast Cards!

5 ARRIVAL AT CAMBRIDGE

Here the Messiah in Trinity; his first meeting with some well-known figures, whose names reading from left to right are Maynard Keynes, Lytton Strachey, Leonard Woolf; They are standing in the Great Court: they are looking at each other in complete silence; which after half an hour was broken by a loud sinister, sonorous portentous groan from the moustache of Lytton.

6 EUPHROSINE (THE SONG BIRDS)

The Messiah encouraging song. Here are depicted, in a circular or Round Robin, Clive, Lytton, Walter Lamb (distinguished by his spherical or egg shaped occiput) & Saxon: dumb.

The outburst of these symphonious voices was caged in a volume, greenish grey and glaucous called Euphrosyne, after the dancing master's daughter.

Still after the roll and ravage of twenty years, say Euphrosyne, whisper the one word in the ear of Clive and he retaliates violently with pellets of bread.[44]

7 THE TWO MISS STEPHENS

Our hero confronted with two heroines – the Stephens sisters to wit, Vanessa (green) Virginia (yellow). Having never met a horse rider, coarse liver, or whiskey drinker the ladies were fascinated by the apparition of him whom they took as such. Hailing him simultaneously with these words

EUPHPRO SENE (THE SONG BIRDS)

THE TWO MISS STEPHENS

F ALLS IN LOVE WITH MISS VANESSA

"What d'you do for ponies broken knees?" They were petrified by the single, monosyllable emphatically pronounced "Keats". Such was the collision & kaleidoscope of two shattered worlds.

8 Falls in love with Miss Vanessa
The archer shot his arrow which struck them in the marrow. As they walked through the gates of Kings.

The marriage
Which took place at St Pancras Registry office, over against the St Pancras workhouse. A motley company felicitated the newly joined; one suicide, two tipsy but jovial charwomen & a navvy called, oddly enough Uppington, the forerunner of one who will figure later. The airy presences include a cherub, an aureole, & a trumpet, lodged in a mouth. Clive's hair played with the sunbeams & shot sunny arrows into Gerald Duckworth's heart.

Arrival at 46 Gordon Square
This is a bald and timid statement of what actually occurred when the newly married arrived at their house. Vans, crates, wagons lorries, cabs, hansom & growler, balloons, captive and escaped, motors, hired & borrowed, sacks, peddlars, packing cases, Pickfords, Carter Pattersons,[45] perambulators – in short anything on wheels or trotters, bowled up to 46 & deposited, heaped, piled, stacked in short dumped down & piled up what was the material foundation of years upon years of miscellaneous family bliss. The door was burst open by the impact of a cast of the Venus of Milo: which disclosed an old woman, & a serried file of the familiar Beetle, commonly, but erroneously styled, Black.

THE MARRIAGE

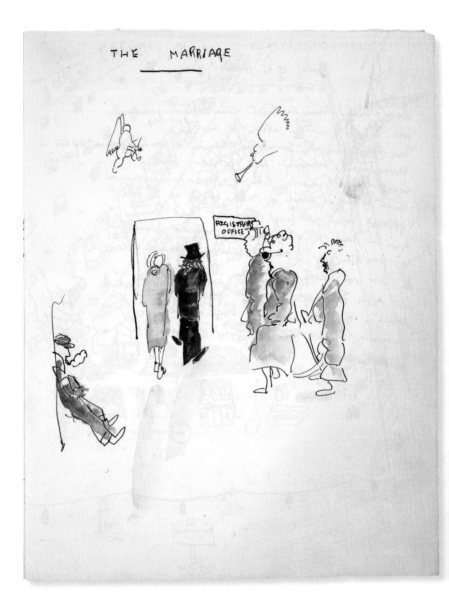

A DINNER PARTY AT 46

Here we have the first entertainment: which comprised reading from left to right, Mrs. Bell, Lytton Strachey, Lord Robert Cecil,[46] Mrs Humphrey Ward, the Quaker & the poet Yeats. Such an assembly had rarely got together & seldom sprung apart. Now they did both.

"Hah" said Mrs. Ward.

"Hum" said the Quaker.

"Huh!" said Lord Robert

& "Tosh!" said Lytton.

The Poet Yeats was not observed to make a single remark, but grinding his teeth, & stamping his feet produced a sound which was expressive of considerable mental equipment in a congealed condition.

HIDING THE MATCH BOX

Every single object in the house was chosen rather for beauty than use; for example the bedroom ware. These leaked: but on the other hand, considered aesthetically, ravished the eye, with their wollops & their scrollops: blue patterns, golden rumps. But the match box! Ah the match box! What could be done to disguise the common Bryant & Mays[47] so that it too should Amaze! For many months Clive pondered & peeved; always striving, never triumphing, for no sooner had he interred or castrated one box than the Haymarket Stores deposited 10 dozen more. We catch him in the climax of his fury, deporting these eyesores, injuries & insults, (to use the mildest opprobria) in the heart of the fire: hence an explosion: a fire; a desolation unspeakable, in which the cat perished, & it is said, a pair of old womens legs. Never mind. Ars Longa; Matchbox Brevis

Nessa and the pram

Mrs. Bell was sometimes abstract in thought; the perambulator did not share this peculiarity: down with rapidity it ran; & there are those who intimate that Julian took on something of his habitual vivacity from this spirited excursion & concussion with the vehicular traffic of the metropolis.

What Clive did in the Great War

"The spade is mightier than the sword" With these words Clive retired to Garsington[48] & dug trenches for turnips; eradicated the thistle; pruned the plum, & then, changing his clouts with the completeness of the Chameleon, tendered, in Lady Ottoline's drawing groom, little cups full of some adulterated form of meat extract.

Intercepted letters

The Hag of the House[49] descended at dawn. First performing those necessary excavations and alterations (such as filling in a wrinkle, decapitating a pimple) which the ravages of a strenuous but unrewarded night made necessary. She lit the tea kettle, watched for a suffusion of steam, & then applied her guests letters to the spout. Removing the contents between thumb & forefinger she proceeded to read – but what?

"Ottoline is a debauched and bedizened hag" at which moment Clive entered, & stuffing the letter between Marie Antoinette's pearls she proceeded to pour out tea: tears and saliva bitter as Dead Sea Salts mingled with the draught.

Shooting a peacock

The kindest of men, to whom the very slugs were sacred, ravaged by hunger and raucous with the din, snatched his gun and shot a peacock. As it died, the voice of the Hag

INTERCEPTED LETTERS

SHOOTING A PEACOCK

sounded with the voice of the bird, & the two shrieks, intertwined in cacophony, writhed and wriggled to Heaven, leaving however Lady Ottoline on earth to jug what remained of the bird's carcase for the evening meal.

The fowl was bred on the parings of her toenails and she cherished for it an almost maternal partiality.

TILLING THE SOIL

But Philip Morrell would find dandelions among the roots, & require their instant extraction, by trowel, before noon. Clive wreaked on these comparatively innocent vegetables a state of heart, mind, guts & gall which had it found a human victim, would speedily have erected another tomb among the ducal tombs at Welbeck.[50] "Ott recovered: t'was the Dand that died".

SICK AT SEA

But why dwell upon the least propitious moments of a hero almost entirely blessed? True, Clive was sick; but equally true, he was never sorry.

As the great sugar factory at Boulogne burst upon his gaze he tossed his cap in the air, struck his breast, and let stream away to the isles of Mexico those black galls & bitter cuds which the Peacocks and Patronesses of Garsington had bred in him.

NEARLY MISTAKEN FOR A FRENCH MAN

At any rate when he landed, the Facteur said to him (in perfect French) words to the effect that had he not been assured of the contrary he would have mistaken Mr. Bell for the legitimate descendant of the great-houses of Bourbon & Valois – a compliment which Clive acknowledged, as the picture shows, by extracting 20 francs from his pocket.

SICK AT SEA

And with these auspicious words our story ends, to begin
again, allowing to the kindness & condescension of our

READERS

TO EACH of whom

we Wish

A HEART OF GOLD

A PURSE OF NOTES

AND A PLATE OF TURKEY.

VIRGINIA AND QUENTIN

Charleston, Christmas, 1925.

Monthly Calendar

1927 January

In the beginning of January the Bell family decided that the climatic conditions of London were unfavourable to their art. Mrs Bell, by advertising in Exchange & Mart discovered a land where there is no conversation, no society, no literature; where the inhabitants are dumb; where the sun always shines from the North; & the old & clear light untainted by intellect & undisturbed by passion which is necessary for the composition of still lives, perpetually prevails. So she packed 87 boxes of canvas & oil paint, let her house to half a dozen coloured gentry of dubious morality & set off one fine winter's day, for Cassis.

She was somewhat dismayed to pass three apparently human beings in the road, but determined not to open her eyes on any provocation whatsoever. She procured a sufficiency of vegetable produce from the town of Marseilles, & arranged enough still lives to last Bell & Grant six months. Then the distinguished couple wetted their brushes & settled in.

February

After three or four weeks of complete silence, the door opened & admitted Colonel Teed.[51] He was followed by Miss Campbell;[52] she by Major Carruthers;[53] he by Wyndham Tryon;[54] next came Miss Bellains [*illeg.*]; finally an American

---

Charleston Bulletin. Vol. xvii. Miscellaneous undated pieces relating to life at Charleston between 1923 and 1927. Loose leaf calendar of events of 1927. By Virginia Woolf, BL Add. 83332.

coal merchant who had lost his wife & had taken to art by way of consolation, edged his way into the room: & were all coldly received.

Unfortunately, there is a flaw in Grant's character. The desire for conversation sometimes seizes him. He articulates not distinctly but rapidly. Soon he was swept into the torrent. The whirlpool, the maëlstrom, of Cassis society. Miss Bellains had him to her bedroom & told him the story of her life. So did Miss Campbell: Mrs. Carruthers; & a lady whose name he never caught. Meanwhile Mrs. Bell, who has no flaw of that kind anywhere about her, had to listen to the adventures & sorrows of the gentlemen. Col. Teed told her he had killed bears in Rangoon. The widower described Mabels death. Though Mrs. B. completely confused the lady & the Bear, her mere presence was a consolation, & it thus fell out that Bell & Grant became the hub of society. No tea party let alone sketching party, to say nothing of little expeditions to the Calangues, or merry gatherings at midnight in Bellains bungalow were complete without them. Wyndham Tryon went mad.

MARCH

Such was the state of affairs when the Woolves arrived. As might have been expected, Mrs. Woolf found extremely congenial society in the company of Mr. Tryon & together they paced the beach by the hour, exchanging ideas often of the highest interest, but unfortunately unintelligible to the rest of the world. Mr. Woolf, whose love of the animal kingdom does him such credit, spent most of his time inducing the frogs to unbosom themselves to him freely. Miss Campbell joined him in this occupation. Meanwhile Mr. Bell wrote his epoch-making work on Civilization on the Balcony.

Mr. Fry fell over a seat & knocked out a tooth, which being his last had a sentimental value. A bird was seen with a snake in its beak. Mrs. Bell prognosticated an omen. No sooner were the words out of her mouth than

APRIL

a telegram arrived What did I say? said Mrs. Bell, "A Catastrophe!" Her eyes lit with joy. "The choice lies between a Renault & a Citroën" she said, letting the telegram fall to the floor. At the same moment the snake fell to the ground. "Grandpapa Bell is dying" she announced, & went into Marseille to choose a car.

MAY

So the grim angel of death hovered over the home of Bell. But nothing as Mrs. Bell said would induce him to settle. The family returned to London; they found coffee coloured stains wherever the Indians had sat down: & life resumed its even way.

The spring was wet in the extreme. At last on a rainy day, the Fowl alluded to above came to perch: & there was perhaps the grandest funeral ever known in Wiltshire.

Violet was sick in the rhododendron bushes. Vanessa Bell met the coffin on the stairs. Quentin struck the right note. All traffic was suspended. The sons carried the pall. Clive opened the Black Box. Vanessa bought a second hand Renault.

JUNE

The less said about this month, the better. Nothing was mentioned except mags: and glass [illeg.]. The only society kept was that of Fred and Harris. The only passions felt were those of rivalry & greed. Clive was forced to desert Bloomsbury in search of Civilisation.

The only question was Citroën or Singer?[55]
Buick or Renault?
Saloon or Touring
Four Cylinder or Six?
+ then the great rivalry began.

July

The less said about July the better.
Mrs. Bell drove from Hyde Pk-Corner to Marble Arch.
Mr. Woolf drove from Marble Arch to Hyde Park Corner.
Mrs. Woolf knocked a boy of his bicycle.
Mrs. Bell killed a cat.
The less said the better.

August

It was discovered that the new study at Tilton was by no means rain-proof.

The discovery was repeated every day between Aug. 1st & Oct. 15th. Nevertheless, the Squire entertained profusely: and was not daunted by the insufficiency of the food & the inadequacy of the liquor from giving several dinner parties. He proved the valuable mathematical fact that two grouse are enough to feed 12 people, allowing for the birds being cooked on toast.

On August 10th the last bottle of so called wine was drunk: & recourse was had to a fine spring of natural water, upon which he had depended ever since.

September

The rain continued, which was welcomed at Tilton; but less so in the alcoholic of the county.

The Renault & the Singer new took the roads together, & it was found unnecessary for either car to use its horn, since

the driver of each never ceased to trumpet the praises of his own conveyance. Cows would stampede at the noise: chickens evaporate: cocks crow.

But impartial observers were unanimously of opinion that the SINGER WAS THE BEST.

OCTOBER

This month was chiefly remarkable for the fact, if such it can be called, that Julian went to Cambridge. But as nobody dares to conceive what he did there we can only have a blank, & hope that it is the white flower of a blameless life.

Old Bloomsbury revived.

One hundred weight of pale surface glass [*illeg.*] was consumed

Maynard's water supply was replenished: Harland[56] was drunk — all efforts to discover on what have failed

NOVEMBER

Imagination boggles at the thoughts of what was said & what was done & over it draws the sheet of pale OBLIVION.

DECEMBER

is thank heaven the last month in the calendar. Nature blinking at what we have had to record drew a white veil over the landscape & did her best to insinuate wine at Tilton: without success.

Among cracked radiators & lunatic motorists, we bow profoundly to the inscrutable will of providence & Take our Leave. Amen!

Biographical notes

Bernard ADENEY (1878–1966), painter and textile designer, and a founding member of the London Artists' Association.

Helen ANREP (1885–1965), née Maitland, studied music in Europe and was associated with the circle of Augustus John and Henry Lamb. In 1917, she married the Russian mosaicist Boris von Anrep who was responsible for the pavements in the entrance hall of the National Gallery, London. From 1926 she lived with Roger Fry until his death. A frequent visitor to Charleston, she was often painted by Vanessa Bell and Duncan Grant.

Barbara BAGENAL (1891–1984) née Hiles, painter, gardener and botanist, studied at the Slade School, 1913–1914, where she made friends with Dora Carrington, and married Nicholas Bagenal in 1918. A visitor to Charleston for over half a century, she was a devotee of Vanessa and Clive Bell, and made several bequests to the Charleston Trust.

Clive BELL (1881–1964), art and literary critic, author of *Civilization* (1928) and *Old Friends* (1956); coined the term 'significant form' in his book *Art* (1914) and supported many of Roger Fry's ideas on aesthetics. He married Vanessa Stephen in 1907 and, although he maintained a separate establishment at 50 Gordon Square, London, during the inter-war years, shared Charleston with Duncan Grant and Vanessa Bell until his death.

Anne Olivier BELL (1916–), née Popham, married Quentin Bell in 1952. Olivier Bell is the editor of *The Diary of Virginia Woolf*, 1915–1941, and serves on the Charleston Trust. She was painted by Vanessa Bell and Duncan Grant.

Quentin Claudian Stephen BELL (1910–1996), younger son of Vanessa and Clive Bell, painter, potter, sculptor, biographer of Virginia Woolf, art historian. He was educated in London and at Leighton Park School. Quentin Bell became lecturer at Newcastle University then professor of art history at Leeds University (1959–1967). During this period he also served as the Slade Professor of Art at Oxford University, and professor of fine art at Hull University. In 1967 he returned to Sussex, where he became professor of art history and theory at the University until his retirement in 1975. He was the first chairman of the Charleston Trust. He married Anne Olivier Bell in 1952 and they had three children: Julian, Virginia and Cressida.

Julian Heward BELL (1908–1937), older son of Vanessa and Clive Bell, writer and poet. Julian Bell was educated at Leighton Park School and King's College Cambridge, where he became an Apostle. He is the author of *Winter Movement* (1930) and he edited *We Did Not Fight: 1914–1918 Experiences of War Resisters* (1935). He taught English at Wuhan University in China in 1935. In 1937 he took part in the Spanish Civil war as an ambulance driver, where he lost his life at the age of 29.

Vanessa ('Nessa') BELL (1879–1961), née Stephen, painter and designer. She designed jackets for the Hogarth Press and for Virginia Woolf's books. A co-director of the Omega Workshops, 1913–1919, with Roger Fry and Duncan Grant, she was between the wars involved in the London Artists' Association and the London Group. The elder daughter of Julia and Leslie Stephen, she married Clive Bell in 1907 and had two sons, Julian and Quentin. After a love affair with Roger Fry, she lived with Duncan Grant, with whom she moved to Charleston in 1916, and had a daughter, Angelica, by him two years later. She lived and worked with Grant there, in France and in London until her death.

Mrs BRERETON, the children's governess, who brought her daughter Anne with her to Charleston. She had been a friend of Roger Fry's and had nursed his wife Helen.

Lord Robert CECIL (1864–1958), lawyer, politician and diplomat, one of the founders of the League of Nations.

Sir Joseph Austen CHAMBERLAIN (1863–1937), statesman and politician, eldest son of Joseph Chamberlain. Leslie Stephen had met Joseph Chamberlain in 1874 and George Duckworth intermittently served as Austen Chamberlain's private secretary. Austen Chamberlain gave Maynard Keynes a lift to Charleston after they had bought a Cézanne and other pictures at the auction of Degas' collection in Paris 1918. (see *A Cézanne in the Hedge*, 138)

Lady Maud "Emerald" CUNARD, née Burke, (1872–1948), American society hostess in London, wife to Sir Bache Cunard, fleetingly mentioned in Virginia Woolf's paper "Am I a snob" and mother of the writer Nancy Cunard. She was also a patron of the Omega. (see *AWD*, 132)

Nancy CUNARD (1896–1965), author and founder of The Hours Press, published the Memories of George Moore and Norman Douglas. She also published her free verse poem with the Hogarth Press. (see *Selected Letters of Vanessa Bell*, 285)

Roger Eliot FRY (1866–1934), art historian, painter and critic. Author of *Vision and Design* (1920) and *Cézanne* (1927). He studied at Cambridge where he became a member of the Apostles. Fry taught art history at the Slade School, was appointed Curator of Paintings at the Metropolitan Museum of Art in New York and Slade Professor at Cambridge in 1933. He put together the Post-Impressionist Exhibitions in 1910 and 1912, and founded the Omega Workshops in 1913.

Lord GAGE (1895–1982), 6th Viscount Gage of Firle Place, owner of Firle Place and landlord to Charleston.

Duncan GRANT (1885–1978), painter and designer, cousin of Lytton Strachey and his numerous siblings, with whom he spent much of his youth. Studied with Jacques-Emile Blanche in Paris before returning to London where he was a co-director of the Omega Workshop and a member of the London Artists' Association and the London Group. Grant persuaded Maynard Keynes to ask the government for money to buy pictures at the Degas sale in Paris in 1917, some of which are in the National Gallery, London. Duncan Grant himself was given two exhibitions at the Tate Gallery during his lifetime. He designed textiles, rugs and embroidery, painted ceramics and furniture, also murals and interior decoration. Grant did woodcuts and illustrations as well as several theatre designs. From 1914 he lived and worked with Vanessa Bell, moving with her in 1916 to Charleston, where in 1918 she gave birth to his daughter Angelica. Although he maintained a London studio, the farmhouse remained his home and principal studio until his death over sixty years later.

Ethel GRANT (1863–1947), née McNeil, wife of Major Bartle Grant (1860–1924) and mother of Duncan Grant. A gifted needlewoman, she carried out designs by Duncan Grant and Vanessa Bell in gros point, several examples of which are to be seen at Charleston.

Mr and Mrs HARLAND, servant and cook, respectively, to the Maynard Keyneses.

(John) Nicholas HENDERSON (1919–2009), diplomat, lastly as British Ambassador to Washington. Stayed at Charleston as one of Majorie Strachey's summer-school pupils.

Grace HIGGENS (1903–1983), née Germany, born in Norfolk, she joined Vanessa Bell's household in 1920 when she was sixteen, finally becoming cook-housekeeper at Charleston, where she lived with her husband, Walter, and son, Peter John, until her retirement in 1970.

Mary Augusta HUMPHREY-WARD (1851–1920), née Arnold, writer and niece of the poet and critic Matthew Arnold, married to Thomas Humphrey Ward fellow and tutor of Brasenose College, Oxford.

Mary HUTCHINSON (1889–1977), née Barnes, a cousin of the Stracheys. Married the barrister St. John Hutchinson in 1910 and later had a long love affair with Clive Bell. Hutchinson was an early visitor to Charleston, a patron of Duncan Grant and Vanessa Bell and the author of *Fugitive Pieces* (1927).

Augustus JOHN (1878–1961), celebrated English portrait painter and brother of Gwen John; met Duncan Grant in Paris in 1907 and Clive and Vanessa Bell shortly afterwards in London; maintained professional relations with Vanessa Bell and Duncan Grant for many years.

John Maynard KEYNES (1882–1946), economist, writer, fellow and Bursar of King's College, Cambridge. The British Treasury's chief representative during the Paris Peace Conference after World War I, he resigned over the settlement being imposed on Germany and wrote *The Economic Consequences of the Peace* (1919) at Charleston, where he was staying as a close friend of Duncan Grant and Vanessa Bell; this was followed by several seminal works on economics. After his marriage in 1925 to Lydia Lopokova, he settled at Tilton, the property neighbouring Charleston; he was created Baron Keynes of Tilton in 1942.

Lydia KEYNES (1892–1981), née Lopokova, Russian ballerina. After training at the Imperial School of Ballet in St. Petersburg, she travelled to London in 1918 with Diaghilev's Ballets Russes and, from 1921, remained at Maynard Keynes's persuasion; she married him four years later, continuing her career on the London stage both as dancer and actress. After Keynes's death she stayed at their home in Tilton, near Charleston, as well as in London and Cambridge.

Henry LAMB (1883–1960), painter; close early friend of Lytton Strachey and Lady Ottoline Morrell and a member of Vanessa Bell's exhibiting society, The Friday Club, from 1905–1908; made pencil drawings of Clive Bell and Duncan Grant and portraits of Strachey and Leonard Woolf.

Edward LE BAS (1904–1966), painter and collector; close friend of Duncan Grant and Vanessa Bell with whom he painted in Europe in 1946 (Dieppe) and in 1955 (Asolo). Owned many works by the two artists and posed for the figure of Christ crucified in Grant's panel in Berwick Church, Sussex.

Nurse LUGTON, a nurse to the Stephen children. "Nurse Lugton's Golden Thimble" a children's story by Virginia Woolf first published in the TLS (17.06.1965), illustrated by Duncan Grant. The story was found in the manuscript for Mrs Dalloway. It was separately published by the Hogarth Press with a foreword by Leonard Woolf.

Desmond MACCARTHY (1877–1952), author, critic and literary editor of New Statesman, 1920–1927, and subsequently senior literary critic on The Sunday Times; president of the English P.E.N. Club; knighted in 1951. With his wife, Molly – they were married in 1906 – a frequent visitor to Charleston, where he was painted by Vanessa Bell and Duncan Grant and sculpted by Quentin Bell.

Mary ('Molly') MACCARTHY (1882–1953), née Warre-Cornish, writer and wife of Desmond MacCarthy, with whom she had three children, Michael, Rachel and David.

MEMOIR CLUB. Met for the first time on 4 March 1920 and continued to the early 1960s; initially composed of members of Old Bloomsbury, who would dine together and hear autobiographical papers read by two or sometimes more members. Meetings usually took place in London with dinner in a restaurant; there were occasional meetings at Charleston and Tilton. For over twenty-five years, from its inception, the Club's secretary was Molly MacCarthy; its last secretary was Frances Partridge. Many papers such as those read by Leonard Woolf, David Garnett and Clive Bell later formed part of their published memoirs.

Lady Ottoline Violet Anne MORRELL (1873–1938), née Cavendish-Bentinck, aristocrat, hostess and influential patroness of the arts. She was closely acquainted with many artists and writers such as Mark Gertler, Aldous Huxley, Roger Fry and T.S. Eliot. Married the MP Philip Morrell in 1902. Their Oxfordshire estate Garsington became a refuge to conscientious objectors such as Clive Bell during the First World War.

Emily PATON, housemaid of Vanessa Bell at Charleston, dismissed for stealing. On her last day, Vanessa Bell reluctantly asked Emily to open her suitcase, and had several bars of soap and a pair of Duncan's trousers flung at her by Miss Paton. (see *Selected Letters of Vanessa Bell*, 30)

(Caroline) Mabel SELWOOD (1893–1989), nurse to Quentin Bell from about 1910–1917.

Beatrice ('Trissy') SELWOOD (1891–1973), sister to Mabel Selwood, sent by Mary Hutchinson to become Vanessa Bell's cook at Charleston in 1917 and was friendly with Virginia Woolf's servants. She married Gerald Stacey, a local landlord, who was himself tenant to Lord Gage in 1918.

Florence Emmeline or 'Flossie' SELWOOD (1887–1987), became nanny to Julian and Quentin Bell after her older sister Elsie. She features in Vanessa Bell's photograph albums. In 1926 Flossie married Edward Weeks, a chauffeur from her home village in Gloucestershire.

Lytton STRACHEY (1880–1932), critic and biographer, author of Eminent Victorians (1918) and Queen Victoria (1921). A cousin of Duncan Grant and a contemporary of Clive Bell at Cambridge, he was among Charleston's favourite visitors, making more or less annual trips there from 1917 onwards.

Marjorie STRACHEY (1882–1962), author and teacher, notably of her summer school at Charleston. One of Lytton's many siblings, she wrote several books, among them Mazzini, Garibaldi and Cavour, which the Hogarth Press published in 1937.

Saxon SYDNEY-TURNER (1880–1962), erudite, musical and taciturn contemporary of Clive Bell, Lytton Strachey and Leonard Woolf at Cambridge and closely associated with early Bloomsbury. A civil servant all his working life, he first visited Charleston in 1917.

Colonel Peter TEED, former Bengal Lancer who had abandoned a wife in India in order to co-habit with an ex-nurse, Jean Campbell, who was a close friend of the New Zealand artist, Frances Hodgkins. Vanessa Bell and Duncan Grant rented their cottage La Bergère in the South of France from Colonel Teed. (see Spalding, Duncan Grant, 278)

Wyndham TRYON (1883–1942), a Slade-trained painter, and member of the New English Art Club living in Cassis. Duncan Grant painted a portrait of Tryon playing his guitar. Tryon's career was terminated by mental illness. During the Second World War, one bomb landed on his studio and another on the depository where many of his paintings were stored. Tryon introduced Duncan Grant to the painter George Bergen. (see Spalding, Duncan Grant, 278, 292)

Mr and Mrs UPPINGTON, the caretakers at Charleston and Gordon Square.

Charles VILDRAC (1882–1964), poet, dramatist and manager of the Galerie Vildrac in Paris, which showed work by Fry, Grant and Bell alongside their French contemporaries; friendship with Fry and the Charleston artists dated from 1911.

Joseph WOLSTENHOLME (1829–1891), mathematician, educated at St. John's College Cambridge and became professor of mathematics at the Royal Indian Engineering College from 1871–1889. Close friend of Leslie Stephen. Wolstenholme served as a model for Augustus Carmichael in *To the Lighthouse*.

Leonard WOOLF (1880–1969), author, editor and publisher. Studied at Trinity College Cambridge, where he was elected an 'Apostle', together with Lytton Strachey, J.M. Keynes, G.E. Moore, E.M. Forster and Bertrand Russell. Worked in the Ceylon Civil Service, 1904–1911, and in the year after his return, married Virginia Stephen; with her, founded The Hogarth Press, publishing among many others Sigmund Freud, T.S. Eliot, E.M. Forster, Vita Sackville-West and Laurens van der Post. Literary editor of *The Nation and Atheneum*, 1923–1929, and on the board of the *New Statesman*, he also wrote two novels and a political work, *After the Deluge* (2 vols., 1931, 1939) – he was, in addition, involved in the League of Nations and various parliamentary committees – and five volumes of autobiography. 'Discovered' Charleston in 1916 while living at Asheham nearby.

Adeline Virginia WOOLF (1882–1941), née Stephen, novelist and critic. Sister of Vanessa Bell, she married Leonard Woolf in 1912 and together they founded The Hogarth Press at Richmond, Surrey, before moving to London. She divided her time between there and Sussex, where she lived first at Asheham, then at Monk's House, Rodmell, both a few miles from Charleston, which she visited frequently with Leonard Woolf, sometimes bringing her own house-guests. She suffered periodic nervous breakdowns, and took her own life in 1941, not long after finishing the last of her nine novels, *Between the Acts*.

Notes and abbreviations

ABBREVIATIONS

CSFVW   *The Complete Shorter Fiction of Virginia Woolf*. Ed. by Susan Dick, 2nd edition, London: Hogarth, 1989.

MOB   *Moments of Being*. Ed. by Jeanne Schulkind, 2nd ed. London: Hogarth, 1985.

HPGN   *Hyde Park Gate News: The Stephen Family Newspaper* [by Virginia Woolf, Vanessa Bell and Thoby Stephen]. Ed. by Gill Lowe, London: Hesperus, 2005.

Letters   *The Letters of Virginia Woolf*. Ed. by Nigel Nicolson and Joanne Trautmann, 6 vols., London: Hogarth, 1975–1980.

D   The *The Diary of Virginia Woolf*. Ed. by Anne Olivier Bell, 5 vols, London: Hogarth, 1977–1984.

INTRODUCTION

1. *The Widow and the Parrot*, illustrated by Julian Bell, Afterword by Quentin Bell (London: Hogarth Press, 1982).
2. *Letters of Virginia Woolf* III, 481.
3. *Letters of Virginia Woolf* III, 492–3.
4. *Letters of Virginia Woolf* III, 292.
5. BL, Add. MS 70725. HPGN.
6. Quentin Bell and Virginia Nicholson. *Charleston. A Bloomsbury House and Garden* (London: Frances Lincoln, 1997), 116.
7. As Anne Olivier Bell, Quentin's widow, notes the 'daily news-sheet, produced by Julian ("The Editor") and Quentin ("The Illustrator") Bell, first appeared on the Charleston breakfast table in the summer holidays in 1923, and survived, as the New Bulletin, until 1927.' 'Footnote', *The Charleston Magazine* 2001, 31.
8. *Charleston. A Bloomsbury House and Garden*, 116.
9. The whereabouts of the Supplement called the Tiltoniad, which Woolf wrote about the Keyneses and spoke of in her letter to Vanessa Bell from August 1927 (Letter 1804, *Letters* III, 415), cannot at present be located.
10. *Selected Letters of Vanessa Bell*, 275.
11. *Letters of Virginia Woolf*, III, 152.
12. *Selected Letters of Vanessa Bell*, 280.
13. *Charleston. A Bloomsbury House and Garden* (London: Frances Lincoln, 1997), 116.

14. *Letters of Virginia Woolf*, III, 452.

15. *Charleston. A Bloomsbury House and Garden*. Preface.

16. *The Letters of Roger Fry*, II, ed. with an introduction by Denys Sutton (London: Chatto & Windus, 1972), to Helen Anrep, 18 April 1925.

17. *Letters of Virginia Woolf*, II, 95.

18. *Selected Letters of Vanessa Bell*, 280

19. Ibid.

20. Frances Partridge, 'Bloomsbury Houses', in: *A Cézanne in the Hedge*, 128–35, 132–3.

21. See also: Richard Shone, *The Art of Bloomsbury. Roger Fry, Vanessa Bell and Duncan Grant* (London: Tate Gallery Publishing, 1999), 32.

TRANSCRIPTS

1. See Virginia Woolf's short story "Nurse Lugton's Golden Thimble", TLS 17.06.1965, which was written for Ann Stephen, daughter of Adrian and Karin Stephen. It is also published under the title "Nurse Lugton's Curtain" in: *CSFVW*, 154–5. See *Diary*, V, 246 (12.11.1939).

2. The Logan Rock is just south of Land's End between Mill Bay and Pendower Coves. The Stephen family visited it during the summers they spent at St. Ives. See *Selected Letters of Leslie Stephen I*, 251.

3. Vanessa losing her mother's umbrella is reported in *HPGN*, 95.

4. Joseph Wolstenholme (30 September 1829–18 November 1891) was an English mathematician. He was a close friend of Leslie Stephen from his undergraduate studies at Cambridge, and a frequent walking companion. Virginia Woolf used his personality for the character Augustus Carmichael in *To the Lighthouse*. See MOB, 73.

5. Lady Margaret Leonora Evelyn Selina Herbert married George Herbert Duckworth on September 10, 1904.

6. George Herbert Duckworth.

7. Virginia Woolf's maternal Aunt Mary Fisher. Woolf, *Letters I*, 163.

8. See Virginia Woolf, *Letters I*, 279. On 8 February 1907 Virginia Woolf wrote to Violet Dickinson describing Vanessa's wedding. 'Wedding successful, - very quick and simple. But Nessa and I got lost going in the Pentonville Rd. And the motor took a short cut so that they missed their train – and had to wait till 12:40. Nessa sent in a line, much amused.'

9. On Vanessa Bell's habit of misquoting or mixing up proverbs see *Deceived with Kindness*, 20: 'such as "It's a long worm that has no turning", or "It's an ill wind that makes the leopard change his spots."'

10. Coastal town in Wales, where Woolf was a summer visitor and wrote parts of *The Waves*.

11. The illustration shows the child Vanessa Bell carrying a chamber pot across a corridor. The Greek key pattern in orange is a reference to patterns used in the Omega Workshop.

12. Mary Augusta Arnold (1851–1920) writer, niece of Matthew Arnold, Aunt of Aldous Huxley, married Thomas Humphrey Ward, fellow and tutor of Brasenose College, Oxford.

13. In 'Old Bloomsbury' Virginia Woolf speaks about Vanessa Bell having charmed Austen Chamberlain (Rosenbaum, *The Bloomsbury Group*, 50). See Biographical notes above.
14. A fellow painter. See Spalding, *Vanessa Bell*.
15. Madame Non-non is still to be identified.
16. A cousin of the Stracheys, Mary Hutchinson (1889–1977) was Clive Bell's long-time companion and lover.
17. This scene still needs to be identified.
18. Mrs. Harland was the cook at Tilton and previously at Gordon Square. See *Deceived*, 50–51.
19. Barbara Bagenal, née Hiles (1891 (?)–1984) married to Nicholas Beauchamp Bagenal (1891–1973) on 1 February 1918. They were divorced in 1951. Children Judith, Henry and Timothy.
    See Letter Vanessa Bell/Maynard Keynes:
    > Barbara seems to mean to spend the summer here in her tent, which may be rather serious if as seems possible she harbours all her & our friends too, but I don't know how one's to prevent anyone who likes from pitching their tent at one's door except by being as unmistakeably hostile as the Woolves – Your VB

    (Monk's House Papers)
20. Trissie, one of Vanessa Bell's servants. See Letters Mary Hutchinson/ Vanessa Bell:
    > Feb. 5th, 1917 (?)
    > Dear Vanessa, Of course I shall be enchanted for you to have Trissie. I think she would suit you extraordinarily well. I am very fond of her and the only thing about her which is slightly annoying is that she varies in character and cooking from day to day. Sometimes she is lovely to look at clean as a new pin cooks like a chef and talks rapidly and gaily. The next day all her hair is down, she is infinitely gruffy can't cook a rice pudding and is in such sulks that no word of any sort can be dragged of her. She adores children which makes me love her. She gives them all the sugar suddenly
    >> You see she is a nice character really and I must say she isn't even sulky

    (Monk's House Papers)
    See Letter Vanessa Bell/Maynard Keynes
    > Charleston, Sept. 11, 1918
    > Dearest Maynard,
    > life has been full of domestic trials & upheavals of every kind since I saw you. This house has been the scene of plots of the Ottoline type & innumerable scenes interviews on the sly mysterious insinuations – till at last I thought I should simply fly. but at last all is settled. Trissie, the Ottoline of this house, leaves on Monday. A temporary woman takes her place for 3 weeks & then Emily's sister comes as permanent cook. Your woman sounds delightful but I don't suppose she'd have come to a country place or she's have been min (?). Clive & Mary come on Tuesday & Duncan's & my plans are that he should tap in his holiday the following Saturday

(Monk's House Papers)

21. See Letters Vanessa Bell/Maynard Keynes,

    Charleston, January 30, 1919

    > Of course domestic crises added to the chaos & in the end Emily left the house without a character [...].

    Charleston, March, 17 (?), 1919

    > a person like Emily was so destructive that I'm also having to restock the house with all she destructed which means most household implements

    (Monk's House Papers)

22. Mr. Hecks was the farmer down the road from Charleston Farmhouse where Duncan Grant and David Garnett served during their conscription.

    See David Garnett's memoir. *The Flowers of the Forest*, 130 f.:

    > Mr. Hecks, my employer, was a suave, dark young man with a pleasant manner. He only paid Duncan and me 12/6 a week and five pence an hour for overtime but he showed great consideration in dealing with us and neither of us ever had a rough word for him. He was married and had a small son. [...] The farm was part of the Gage estate and only about 120 acres in extent but Mr. Hecks had just taken another farm called Lower Tilton, nearer to Charleston, as well.

23. Alice Uppington, the caretaker's daughter.

24. Mrs. Uppington, the charwoman and caretaker's wife.

25. This refers to Lord Gage, Viscount Gage of Firle Place (1895–1982).

26. Henry Winsor and William Newton founded this shop selling paint and artist materials in 1832 at 38 Rathbone Place, London.

27. John Ruskin's essay *The Seven Lamps of Architecture* (1849) received the approval of the Cambridge Camden Society and was well known among Bloomsbury artists.

28. Mr and Mrs Uppington were the caretakers at Charleston. See Virginia Woolf, *Letters* IV, 331.

29. Mr William Ford is yet to be identified.

30. This title pun refers to Alexander Pope's satirical poem *The Dunciad*, the first three books of which were published in 1728, the fourth in 1743.

31. The *Mary Celeste*, a US ship found abandoned in the Atlantic in December 1872 with sails set and evidence of recent occupation, has become synonymous with unsolved mystery.

32. This event is recorded in *Charleston. A Bloomsbury House and Garden*, 111.

33. The seat of The Doune, the Grants' country estate in the foothills of the Cairngorm Mountains.

34. A coloured piece of quartz. See *CSFVW*, 118.

35. This episode refers to an incident in Duncan Grant's youth, when his uncle Trevor told Bartle Grant about having found a rather explicit book about the adventures of young ladies in Duncan's drawer. Bartle arranged for Duncan Grant to be seen by Dr. Hyslop the head of Bedlam who assured Duncan that there was nothing wrong with him. See Spalding, *Duncan Grant*, 29–31.

See Letters Duncan Grant/Virginia Woolf: 23. September 1912. (Monk's House Papers U of Sussex)

Duncan Grant told Virginia Woolf that he almost believed 'that uncle Trevor was right and that I shall end my days in the Royal Bethlem Hospital surrounded by hundreds of unfinished works'. See Spalding, *Duncan Grant*, 125.

36. Virginia Woolf refers to this event in "Old Bloomsbury" (Rosenbaum, *The Bloomsbury Group*, 56): "He borrowed old china from us to paint, and my father's trousers to go to parties in. He broke the china and he ruined the trousers by jumping into the Cam to rescue a child who was swept into the river by the rope of Walter Lamb's barge, the Aholibah".

37. See Hussey, *Virginia Woolf A-Z*, 64. Lady Cunard (née Burke) (1872–1948), society hostess, famous patron of the Omega, and mother of the writer Nancy Cunard.

38. Rose Vildrac, wife of Roger Fry's friend the poet Charles Vildrac. Virginia Woolf, *Roger Fry*, 206.

39. Bernard Adeney (1878–1966) was a former president of the London Group. See *Selected Letters of Vanessa Bell*, 296: "Roger ought to be pleased, for next to Duncan he had sold most – 7. I sold 6. [Frederick] Porter 5. Adeney I think 3 and Keith only 2 – at least that was the last report".

40. For Quentin Bell's description of this incident in another issue of the *Charleston Bulletin* see BL Add. 83317:

Aug. 19th

Duncan sets the Pond on Fire

On Sunday the Bughunters with Duncans aid made a campaign against the weed on the pond. The bug hunters began in the middle of the afternoon and Duncan joined in after tea many experiments were made. Duncan for instance tried setting the pond on fire with petrol but no weed was killed in this way.

41. See Virginia Woolf, *Diary III*, 16: 'Leonard is giving Randall his farewell dinner'. John Randall had served as a proof-reader on *The Nation and Atheneum* for 50 years in 1925. (see *Diary III*, 16, n.5)

42. John Nicholas Henderson, literary editor of *The Nation and Atheneum*. See Virginia Woolf, *Letters III*, 47; *Diary III*, 80; *Diary I*, 3.5.1918.

43. This refers to Henry Somerset, 9th Duke of Beaufort (1847–1924), whose hunt included parts of Wiltshire.

44. Euphrosyne: a privately published collection of poetry by Cambridge friends that was compiled by Clive Bell in 1905.

45. British road haulage firms.

46. Lord Robert Cecil (1864–1934), lawyer, politician and diplomat, one of the founders of the League of Nations.

47. Company founded after 1861 to produce matches in Bow, London.

48. Garsington Manor, the Oxfordshire home of Lady Ottoline Morrell.

49. I.e. Lady Ottoline Morrell.

50. Welbeck Abbey, Nottinghamshire, the house of the Duke of Portland and the family home of Lady Ottoline Morrell, née Cavendish-Bentinck.

51. Colonel Peter Teed. See Spalding, *Duncan Grant*, 278; *Deceived*, 67. Vanessa

Bell and Duncan Grant rented their cottage near Cassis, La Bergère, from Colonel Teed.

52. Jean Campbell, former nurse, living with Colonel Teed, close friend of the New Zealand Artist Frances Hodgkins. See Spalding, *Duncan Grant*, 278.

53. Still to be identified.

54. Wyndham Tryon. See Spalding, *Duncan Grant*, 276; 278; 292. English painter who lived in Cassis. Duncan Grant painted a portrait of him. Tryon's career was terminated by mental illness and his works destroyed by bombs.

55. The Bells had bought a Renault, the Woolfs a Singer. Quentin Bell speaks about their rivalry in *Elders and Betters*, 114.

56. Mr Harland was Maynard Keynes's manservant. Mrs Harland was the cook.

Select bibliography

Anscombe, Isabelle. *Omega and After*. London: Thames & Hudson, 1981.

Bell, Alan (ed.). *Sir Leslie Stephen's Mausoleum Book*. Oxford: Clarendon Press, 1977.

Bell, Quentin and Nicholson, Virginia. *Charleston. A Bloomsbury House and Garden*. London: Frances Lincoln, 1997.

Bell, Clive. *Old Friends: Personal Recollections*. London: Chatto & Windus, 1956.

Bell, Quentin. *Bloomsbury*. London: Weidenfeld & Nicolson, new ed. 1986.

———, *Elders and Betters*. London: John Murray, 1995.

———, *Virginia Woolf*. London: The Hogarth Press, 1972.

Bell, Quentin and Angelica Garnett. *Vanessa Bell's Family Album*. London: Jill Norman and Hobhouse Ltd., 1981.

Bell, Quentin, Angelica Garnett, Henrietta Garnett, Richard Shone. *Charleston Past and Present*. London: The Hogarth Press, 1987.

Bell, Anne Olivier, 'Footnote', *The Charleston Magazine*. Charleston, Bloomsbury and the Arts. Autumn/Winter, 2001. 31–36.

Bradshaw, David, 'Those Extraordinary Parakeets: Clive Bell and Mary Hutchinson. Part One', *Charleston Magazine*, 16 (Autumn/Winter 1997), pp. 5–12.

Bradshaw, David, 'Those Extraordinary Parakeets: Clive Bell and Mary Hutchinson. Part Two', *Charleston Magazine*, 17 (Spring/Summer 1998), pp. 5–11.

Collins, Millie. *Bloomsbury in Sussex*. Albourne: Albourne Publications, 1990.

Charleston Guide Notes, published by the Charleston Trust, 1996.

The Charleston Magazine: Charleston, Bloomsbury and the Arts, published by the Charleston Trust, nos 1–15, 1990–1997.

The Charleston Newsletter ed. Hugh Lee, nos 1–24, published by the Charleston Trust 1982–1989.

Curtis, Vanessa. *The Hidden Houses of Virginia Woolf and Vanessa Bell*. London: Robert Hale, 2005.

Dell, Marion and Marion Whybrow, *Virginia Woolf & Vanessa Bell: Remembering St. Ives*. Padstow: Tabb House, 2004.

Dunn, Jane. *A Very Close Conspiracy: Vanessa Bell and Virginia Woolf*. London: Jonathan Cape, 1990.

Garnett, Angelica. *Deceived with Kindness*. London: Hogarth Press, Chatto & Windus, 1984. Oxford Paperbacks, 1985.

Garnett, Angelica. "Charleston Remembered", *The Antique Collector*, vol. 57, no. 5 (1986), 68.

Garnett, David. *The Flowers of the Forest*. London: Chatto & Windus, 1955.

Harris, Alexandra. *Virginia Woolf*. London: Thames & Hudson, 2011.

Humm, Maggie. *Snapshots of Bloomsbury. The Private Lives of Virginia Woolf and Vanessa Bell*. London: Tate, 2006.

Hussey, Mark, *Virginia Woolf A–Z: A Comprehensive Reference for Students, Teachers and Common Readers to Her Life, Work and Critical Reception*, New York: Facts on File, 1995.

Hyde Park Gate News. The Stephen Family Newspaper. Virginia Woolf, Vanessa Bell with Thoby Stephen. Ed. with an Introduction and Notes by Gill Lowe. London: Hesperus, 2005.

Lee, Hermione. *Virginia Woolf*. New York: Random House, 2010 [1996].

Lee, Hugh (ed.). *A Cézanne in the Hedge*. London: Collins and Brown, 1992.

The Letters of Roger Fry, II. Ed. with an introduction by Denys Sutton. London: Chatto & Windus, 1972.

Light, Alison. *Mrs. Woolf and the Servants*. London: Penguin, 2007.

MacWeeney, Alen, and Sue Allison. *Bloomsbury Reflections*. New York: W.W. Norton; London: Ryan, 1990.

Maitland, Frederic W. *The Life and Letters of Leslie Stephen*. London: Duckworth & Co, 1906.

Marler, Regina (ed.). *Selected Letters of Vanessa Bell*. London: Bloomsbury, New York: Pantheon, 1993.

Naylor, Gillian (ed.). *Bloomsbury: The Artists, Authors and Designers by Themselves*. London: Reed Consumer Books, 1990.

d' Offay, Anthony. *The Omega Workshops: Alliance and Enmity in English Art 1911–1920*. London, 1984.

d'Offay, Anthony. *In Celebration of Charleston*. London, 1986. (no. 22)

Olk, Claudia. 'Virginia Woolf's Art of Scene-Making in the Charleston Bulletin Supplements', *Literature Compass*: Selected Proceedings of the 15th Annual Conference on Virginia Woolf, Oxford: Blackwell, 4:1 (2007), 252–63.

Rosenbaum, S.P. (ed.). *The Bloomsbury Group*. Toronto: University of Toronto Press, 1995.

Shone, Richard. *Bloomsbury Portraits*. London: Phaidon, 1993.

Skidelsky, Robert. *John Maynard Keynes* (2 vols) London: Macmillan, 1983, 1992.

Spalding, Frances. *Vanessa Bell*. London: Weidenfeld & Nicolson, 1983.

———. *Duncan Grant*. London: Chatto & Windus, 1997.

Stansky, Peter and William Abrahams. *Journey to the Frontier. Julian Bell and John Cornford: Their Lives and the 1930s*. London: Constable, 1966.

Stansky, Peter. *On or About December 1910: Early Bloomsbury and Its Intimate World*. Cambridge MA: HUP, 1996.

Sutton, Denys (ed.). *Letters of Roger Fry* (2 vols). London: Chatto & Windus, 1972.

Todd, Dorothy, Raymond Mortimer, *The New Interior Decoration*, London: Batsford, 1929.

Watney, Simon. *The Art of Duncan Grant*. London: John Murray, 1990.

Woolf, Virginia. *Between the Acts*. Cambridge: Cambridge University Press, 2012. [1941]

————. *Collected Essays I–IV*. London: Hogarth Press, 1966–1967.

————. *The Complete Shorter Fiction of Virginia Woolf*. Ed. by Susan Dick. The Hogarth Press, 1985. Revised and enlarged edition, San Diego/New York: Harcourt, 1989.

————. *The Diary of Virginia Woolf* I-V. Ed. by Anne Olivier Bell. London: The Hogarth Press, 1977–1984.

————. *The Letters of Virginia Woolf* I-VI. Ed. by Nigel Nicolson and Joanne Trautmann. New York/London: Harcourt Brace Jovanovich, 1975–1980.

————. *To the Lighthouse*. New York, London: Harcourt Brace Jovanovich, 1989 [1927].

————. *Mrs. Dalloway*. Harmondsworth: Penguin, 1992 [1925].

————. *Orlando*. Ed. by J.H. Stape. Oxford: Blackwell, 1994 [1929].

————. *Roger Fry. A Biography*. New York, London: Harcourt Brace Jovanovich, 1976 [1940].

————. *The Waves*. London: Vintage, 2000 [1931].

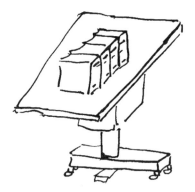

Acknowledgements

It HAS BEEN a great pleasure to work on the *Charleston Bulletin Supplements*. I shall always be grateful to Chris Fletcher, who introduced me to the manuscripts. I have enjoyed working with the editors Lara Speicher and David Way at British Library Publishing and would like to thank them for their advice, and their exceptional help and proficiency. Various institutions have supported my research: I would like to express my gratitude to the Alexander von Humboldt Foundation for awarding me a Feodor Lynen Fellowship, and Rector Frances Cairncross and the Governing Body of Exeter College Oxford for granting me a research fellowship. My special thanks go to Helen Watanabe O'Kelly for all her support and generosity.

I am also indebted to the British Library, the Tate Archive, the University of Sussex Archives, and the Charleston Trust, who all granted me access to their collections. I am very grateful to Anne Olivier Bell and to Jeremy Crow from the Society of Authors for their help and permission to publish the Supplements.

I had the privilege of discussing my work with a number of colleagues and friends, and would like to thank them for their support and inspiration: Nicola Achterberg, Christoph Bode, David Bradshaw, Sally Brown, Hans Walter Gabler, Jeri Johnson, Tom and Susan Kohut, Thomas Lange, Verena Lobsien, Daniela Mairhofer, Bernfried Nugel, Klaus Ostheeren, Hermann Josef Real, Frances Spalding and Sarah Stanton. To Christian, who lived with this project over the years and on different continents, as ever, my love and thanks.

Cambridge, Massachusetts, March 2013